RACHAEL RAY

TOP CHEFS

OTHER TITLES IN THIS SERIES:

ALTON BROWN

PAULA DEEN

BOBBY FLAY

EMERIL LAGASSE

WOLFGANG PUCK

GORDON RAMSAY

TOP CHEFS

RACHAEL RAY

SUSAN KORMAN

Produced by OTTN Publishing, Stockton, New Jersey

Eldorado Ink
PO Box 100097
Pittsburgh, PA 15233
www.eldoradoink.com

CPSIA compliance information: Batch#TC010112-7. For further
information, contact Eldorado Ink at info@eldoradoink.com.

First printing

1 3 5 7 9 8 6 4 2

Library of Congress Cataloging-in-Publication Data

Korman, Susan.
 Rachael Ray / by Susan Korman.
    p. cm. — (Top chefs)
 Includes bibliographical references and index.
 ISBN 978-1-61900-025-4 (hc)
 ISBN 978-1-61900-026-1 (pb)
 ISBN 978-1-61900-027-8 (ebook)
1. Ray, Rachael—Juvenile literature. 2. Cooks—United
States—Biography—Juvenile literature. 3. Celebrity chefs—United
States—Biography—Juvenile literature. I. Title.
 TX649.R29K67 2012
 641.5092—dc23
 [B]
                              2011044851

For information about custom editions, special sales, or
premiums, please contact our special sales department at
info@eldoradoink.com.

TABLE OF CONTENTS

This photograph of Rachael Ray was taken around the time that she first drew national attention for her cooking demonstration on the Today show.

CHAPTER ONE

A STAR IS BORN!

It was Friday, March 2, 2001, and a massive blizzard was threatening the East Coast of the United States. Based on their computer models, weather forecasters were predicting that an historic "monster" storm was on its way.

At the New York City offices of the *Today* show, a national morning news program, producers were worried. With the threat of heavy snow, many of the show's scheduled guests were cancelling their appearances for the following week, saying they were unable to travel to New York. That was when one of the show's producers remembered a substitute guest recently suggested by Al Roker, a popular weatherman and host for *Today*. The name of that substitute was Rachael Ray, a cook whom Roker had seen doing segments on a local TV station in upstate New York where he had a vacation home. Her TV segments were called "30-Minute Meals with Rachael Ray." Rachael Ray was an unknown, but she was young and attractive with an appealing, self-deprecating sense of humor. Roker had a hunch that she'd make an enter-taining guest on *Today*.

"She was just this really cute girl . . . very natural . . . just was who she was," Roker recalled about the first time he saw Rachael on TV. "She is the epitome of what [my mentor] Willard Scott always told me was the best bit of advice, 'Be yourself.'"

When the phone rang that day inside Rachael's cabin in Lake Luzerne, a small town in upstate New York, her mother, Elsa Scudieri, was in the kitchen. And when she picked up the phone and heard who was calling, she couldn't believe her ears. The *Today* show was calling to invite Rachael to appear on the show?

Doing cooking segments on TV wasn't Rachael's only job. To make ends meet, she was also demonstrating cooking tech-niques at several different Price Chopper stores, a local gro-cery chain in upstate New York. When Rachael was paged in the meat department at one of the stores, and then heard why her mother was calling, she couldn't believe the news either. She was convinced that the call was somebody's idea of a joke! But to her amazement, when she dialed the phone number her mother had given her, someone at the *Today* show answered.

"I was so scared when they actually answered the phone," Rachael remembered. "I had to hang up!" She took a few minutes to calm herself down and then she called back, eagerly agreeing to come to New York City to tape the show. Her assignment? To prepare six hearty soups for weatherman Al Roker. After hanging up the phone, Rachael called her mother back. Elsa remembers Rachael squealing in excite-ment, "Al Roker! The *Today* Show!"

The following Monday, Rachael and her mother packed up the car with pots and pans and other cooking supplies, then left for Manhattan. The drive from upstate New York normally took about four hours, but by now the predicted snowstorm had arrived in upstate New York. Snow quickly accumulated on the ground, and strong winds blowing the

THE TODAY SHOW

When NBC News launched the *Today* show on January 14, 1956, NBC became the first of the three major networks to have a morning news program. This was especially significant before the days of cable television, when ABC, CBS, and NBC dominated the airwaves. Soon after *Today*'s launch, both CBS and ABC developed morning news shows of their own.

In 2001, Today *show weatherman Al Roker suggested that then-unknown Rachael Ray would make a good guest for the popular morning program.*

Today is now the fourth-longest-running television series. In its early days, *Today* even had a funny and popular mascot—a chimpanzee named J. Fred Muggs. Now the show blends lifestyle segments and lighter news with more serious information. Occasionally it has the opportunity to deliver breaking news about important events, such as Hurricane Katrina in 2005 or the September 11 terrorist attacks on the World Trade Center in 2001. *Today* was launched as a two-hour program, but over time, two more hours were added. Some recent hosts have included Katie Couric, Matt Lauer, Meredith Viera, Ann Curry, and weathermen Willard Scott and Al Roker.

flakes made it hard to see the road. By the time Rachael and her mom finally arrived in the city—about nine hours later—Rachael had time for just a few hours of sleep before heading to the *Today* studios early the next morning to start preparing the soups.

Luckily for Rachael, a lot of people had stayed home from work and school that day because of the weather forecast. Her segment aired with millions of viewers watching. Many of them, including Al Roker, were charmed by her casual, down-to-earth approach in the kitchen. Rachael was funny as she cooked, cracking jokes, dropping things, and hacking vegetables more like a regular home cook than the professionally trained chefs who usually appeared on *Today*. She later joked about what happened when Roker tried to sample something she was making: "Of all the soups I made, Al decided to taste the chicken soup, which wasn't fully cooked. I was thinking, 'Great, I'm about to kill Al Roker on national TV.'"

But none of Rachael's kitchen blunders that day mattered at all. *Today* producer Michele Leone was "smiling from ear to ear" when the segment was over, delighted that everything

The "historic" snowstorm predicted for early March 2001 may have launched Rachael Ray's career, but otherwise it was remembered more as the storm that wasn't. Parts of New England and upstate New York did in fact receive a lot of snow, but much less fell in New York City and Connecticut than meteorologists had originally predicted. Meanwhile, many schools, businesses, and major highways had been closed in response to the erroneous predictions.

had gone so well and amused by Rachael's goofy, girl-next-door manner. Rachael was a little more critical of herself, worriedly asking her mother if she'd said the word "groovy" too many times. The whole experience felt surreal, like a "fairy tale," she said later. As she was standing there next to Al Roker, demonstrating how to make chicken dumpling soup, all she could think was, "What am I doing here? I am a waitress from upstate New York, what qualification do I have to be showing all of America how to make soup?"

Deep down, however, Rachael knew that her first appearance on national TV—in front of "all of America"—had gone smoothly. In fact, it had gone better than that. The emergency substitute guest from the little town in upstate New York had been a huge hit. In the midst of the March 2001 snowstorm, a new culinary star had been born. That new star had never gone to culinary school or had any kind of formal training in the kitchen—but she was about to transform food TV, the cookbook industry, and the lives of millions of home cooks.

CHAPTER TWO

GROWING UP

Rachael Domenica Ray was born on August 25, 1968, on Cape Cod in Massachusetts. She had an older sister, Maria, and would later have a younger brother, Emmanuel ("Manny"). Rachael's parents, Elsa Scudieri and James Ray, owned three busy restaurants on the Cape.

Instead of leaving the three children at home while she was working, Rachael's mom often brought them along to work with her. As Rachael related in a *New York Times* interview, "Rachael Ray Wants Kids in the Kitchen," this experience deeply influenced her feelings and thoughts about food:

> [My mom] brought us to work with her, so either in a commercial production kitchen or a home kitchen, I was always on her hip or at the counter or at her side. There is such a great lesson to learn in having your children in the kitchen with you. Children can smell the smells and watch all that goes into the preparation of the food. It's a five-sense experience for them.

New York's Adirondack Mountains rise over scenic Lake George in this autumn photograph. When Rachael was growing up, her family lived in the nearby town of Lake Luzerne. Nicknamed the "Gateway to the Adirondacks," Lake Luzerne is a small town with a population of about 3,000.

Rachael says she learned how to be a good storyteller from her father; she also learned to love spicy Cajun and Creole dishes from his native state, Louisiana. Her first word was *vino*, which is Italian for "wine," and one of her earliest memories was set in the kitchen. "My first vivid memory is watching my mom in a restaurant kitchen," she recalled. "She was flipping something with a spatula. I tried to copy her and ended up grilling my right thumb! I was 3 or 4." In the introduction to one of her

Rachael's favorite foods when she was a kid were things that her grandfather liked—sardines, squid, and anything with garlic and oil.

cookbooks, *Cooking Rocks! Rachael Ray 30-Minute Meals for Kids*, Rachael described how her mother would "play music and hum and dance around the kitchen . . . while she moved mountains, platters, and pots full of food!"

According to her mother, Rachael was a happy and curious child. "The minute she was up, she wanted to be where you were," Elsa said in an interview for *Vanity Fair* magazine. "And whatever was happening, she wanted to be around that."

A SPECIAL RELATIONSHIP

Rachael also spent a lot of time with her grandfather, Emmanuel Scudieri, who lived with the family for a while when Rachael was young. He often babysat for Rachael and her siblings. A Sicilian emigrant and stonecutter who adored Rachael, Emmanuel was the one who had taught Rachael's mom—the oldest daughter of ten children—how to cook many years before. Rachael says that when Emmanuel was cooking, usually preparing pasta dishes or cooking meat or fish and fresh vegetables, the house smelled like "good food . . . garlic and oil." He often prepared foods from Sicily, an island in Italy that's known for its delicious fresh fruits and vegetables and excellent cuisine. Rachael also remembers that her doting grandfather would often let her dip a finger into the pot to taste whatever was cooking that day. That was a little different from her mother, who tended to be stricter with the kids in the kitchen.

It seems that Rachael inherited more than her grandfather's love of cooking. According to family members, Emmanuel also passed along to his granddaughter his wide, easy smile and enthusiastic appreciation of life.

IN SCHOOL

As a young girl, Rachael was frequently ill with croup, a respiratory illness that causes swelling of the vocal chords and a barking cough. For Rachael, that meant huddling under a vaporizing tent made out of sheets and a broomstick, so that she could breathe in steam to clear her cough. She spent many hours in bed, drawing and daydreaming. She also liked to write. Her mother described Rachael sitting on the floor, "drawing something or writing something. She was always doing that."

CROUP

Rachael has an unusually husky-sounding voice, probably the result of her many childhood bouts of croup. This illness is common in infants and children and can be caused by a virus, bacteria, or allergies.

Croup usually starts with cold-like symptoms and then develops into a cough that sounds like a barking seal. The coughing is often worse at night and can last for almost a week. Years ago, before children were routinely immunized and before antibiotics were widely available, croup was considered a deadly disease, one greatly feared by parents. Today most cases of croup are mild, but it can still become serious, especially in infants and very young children.

At school, Rachael also showed talent in writing and drawing. But when lunchtime rolled around, it was a different story. "I had the lunchbox that cleared the cafeteria," she joked later in a *People* magazine story. "Because I hung out with my grandfather, I started to bring . . . sardine sandwiches and calamari that I would eat off my fingers like rings. I was also always reeking of garlic!" Still, Rachael insisted she wasn't lonely at lunchtime. "I sat alone, but that's okay," she said. "I sat alone with good food!"

As a young girl she took dance lessons, although according to a family story related in *Vanity Fair*, she didn't enjoy practicing much. "I don't want to do any more exercises," she told her parents. "I [just] want to dance."

FAMILY CHANGES—AND A YOUNG COOK

In the early 1970s, Rachael's family moved from Cape Cod to Lake Luzerne, a small town in the Adirondacks in upstate New York. Her father had a new job working for a publishing company while her mother stayed in the food business, managing nine restaurants that were part of a large chain. Watching Elsa train new employees, plan menus, and solve whatever problems came up during the hectic days at the restaurants, Rachael learned a lot about hard work and dedication. In fact, her hardworking mother has always been one of her heroes.

It's easy to guess that Rachael's favorite color is orange. Many of her kitchen products and cookbooks—including one called *Rachael Ray's Big Orange Book*—have featured that color.

"I'm a pale comparison next to her," Rachael recounted on the news show *20/20*. "My mother worked 100 hours a week, and wouldn't bat an eyelash. All my life she was iconic to me, she was my first Oprah. . . . She was like the person I looked at, and I said, 'Wow.'"

Her mother's job also enabled Rachael to observe many things about the food business—how to prepare food for groups of people, serve customers, and manage a restaurant. Rachael often filled in for dishwashers and waitresses who called in sick. "I was surrounded by all different styles of cooking," she recalled, "and worked in the food service industry in just about every capacity you can imagine."

By age twelve, Rachael had learned enough about food preparation to create her first original meal: lasagna roll-ups served with a Gorgonzola sauce and accompanied by asparagus, which Rachael carefully arranged on the plate in a perfect fan shape. Her brother and sister had grown up to enjoy cooking, too. Even today the family says that Maria is the best at baking, while Manny likes to slow cook. Rachael, on the other hand, has always excelled at "canoodling" recipes—taking complicated recipes and making them easier to prepare.

All of these food experiences, both at home and in professional kitchens, led Rachael to form very strong feelings about the importance of kids helping in the kitchen, as she wrote in her introduction to *Cooking Rocks!*:

> The kitchen was the center of my childhood home. As kids, my brother and sister and I were spoiled in an unusual way. We were treated as respected members of the group . . . [and] we were made to feel confident in our own abilities. We felt a responsibility to figure out how to do things for ourselves.

> Rachael didn't learn to drive until she was in her late twenties. Even then, it took her a while to feel comfortable behind the wheel.

When Rachael was thirteen, her parents divorced. But the divorce wasn't bitter, and it didn't change Rachael's view of her childhood as a happy one. In fact, Rachael would later describe the divorce in positive terms: "For us, it made for a happier family."

Rachael attended Lake George High School, a very small school where she was a cheerleader for the Lake George Warriors. She was 5'4" and apparently quite fearless when it came to doing the more daring cheers. In an interview with the *Seattle Post-Intelligencer*, she declared she was the "ta-da

Rachael (center) was a cheerleader while a student at Lake George High School.

cheerleader, the one who climbed to the top of the pyramid and then flipped into the arms of other cheerleaders."

As reporter Kim Severson wrote in a *New York Times* article, "Being Rachael Ray: How Cool is That?," Rachael always had lots of ideas and was looking for new opportunities. While she was still a teenager, she wrote to the founder of the J. Peterman Company because she liked their catalog so much. She even became pen pals with New Orleans district attorney Harry Connick, Sr., after writing to him in hopes that he would arrange for his famous son, jazz musician Harry Connick, Jr., to attend a Saratoga Springs jazz and supper club she wanted to open.

Rachael also saw an opportunity to start her own business when she was still in high school. It was called "Delicious Liaisons" and involved selling gift baskets stuffed with packaged food items such as pasta and cocoa. Rachael hand-lettered and decorated the catalog for the business on her own.

When she graduated from Lake George High School in 1986, Rachael's classmates voted her "most artistic." A few months later, she headed off to Pace University, a small college just north of New York City. She had decided to study literature and communications, but she was uncertain about her long-term career goals. She knew she was talented in art, writing, food service, and cooking, but what could she do with these skills?

Pace University is a private institution that was founded in 1906. It has approximately 8,000 undergraduate students and campuses in lower Manhattan, midtown Manhattan, and Westchester County in New York.

In 1991, Rachael took a job at the candy counter of Macy's department store, located in midtown Manhattan's Herald Square. Her hard work and outgoing personality impressed her bosses and soon earned her a promotion.

CHAPTER THREE

30-Minute Meals and More

When Rachael started taking classes at Pace University, it was the first time she had been away from her family for an extended period. This was a very big change for Rachael, who was close to her mother and siblings Maria and Manny. Although she was enrolled at Pace as a full-time student, she also worked nearly forty hours a week, waitressing at various restaurants and continuing to make baskets for her business Delicious Liaisons.

After two years of attending classes at Pace University, though, Rachael decided it was time to take a break from school. The tuition was expensive, and she was still unsure about her career goals. "It felt . . . like I was going to school for hobbies," she shared in *Vanity Fair*. "I didn't know what I wanted to do." She decided to work and save money while figuring out what she wanted to do with her life.

In 1991 Rachael saw an ad in the *New York Times* for a job at Macy's Marketplace, which was the food department of the busy department store in Manhattan. The position was for a manager of the candy counter. The idea of selling fine chocolates and other gourmet treats instantly appealed to Rachael. Every year her family had traveled to Manhattan at Christmas to see the sights and tour the famous toy store FAO Schwartz. As a young girl, Rachael had often imagined herself working in New York City, where surely something magical was bound to happen. "I saw this little ad in *The New York Times* for a candy-counter manager at Macy's," she later said, "and I thought, 'Well I could do that.'"

When she applied for the job, Rachael's funny answers and obvious work ethic won over Michael Corsello, the man who interviewed her for the position. Corsello hired her on the spot. Soon Rachael was on her way to starting a new life in New York City.

IN THE BIG APPLE

Rachael moved into an apartment in Queens, New York. When she began her new job, Rachael didn't disappoint her boss. She was funny and interacted easily with the customers who shopped at the candy counter. So when the fresh foods manager at Macy's Marketplace left shortly after Rachael was hired, Corsello offered Rachael that job. He said it would only be on a temporary basis until he could find a more experienced replacement.

Macy's at Herald Square in Manhattan covers an entire city block! It was built in 1902 and was the first building to have a modern-day escalator. Shoppers still use those original wooden escalators today.

But Rachael leaped in, quickly taking on lots of extra responsibility. She worked harder than ever before, learning about gourmet foods such as smoked salmon, imported cheeses, coffee, and fancy varieties of olive oil and vinegar. Corsello and others at Macy's were so impressed by her strong work ethic that they ultimately decided to let her keep the fresh foods position.

Two years later, in 1993, another opportunity arose at the store, this one in the women's clothing department. Rachael was offered a chance to train to be a buyer of accessories such as hats, scarves, and jewelry. But this time Rachael wasn't interested in a promotion. During her time at Macy's Marketplace, she had learned something very important about herself: she loved working with food. That was what she wanted to spend her career doing. She turned down the promotion, knowing that it was time to look for a new job.

AGATA & VALENTINA

Rachael soon landed a spot at a new gourmet food store that was opening in an upscale neighborhood on the Upper East Side of Manhattan. It specialized in high-quality Sicilian food and wine and was named after the owner's wife, Agata, and their daughter, Valentina. Rachael instantly felt at home in the shop and with the owners, the Musco family, who were Sicilian like Rachael. In fact, they felt such a strong connection that Rachael's initial interview lasted for hours!

As the manager at Agata & Valentina, Rachael helped customers purchase wine, homemade pastas, cheeses and meats imported from Italy, dessert pastries, and pantry items such as spices, chutneys, and other condiments. The store also sold prepared foods such as sandwiches, roasted

meats and vegetables, and gelato. She worked hard and con-
tributed a lot to the store, something that was noticed and
appreciated by the owners and other staff members. "We
had a problem with the slicer, she went and fixed it," Joe
Musco recalled when describing Rachael as an employee.
"We had a problem with the cash register, she was good at
electronics. . . . She had everybody's respect because she
learned [how to do everything]."

As she served customers in the store, Rachael continued
to expand her knowledge of gourmet foods. At the same time
she was gaining a very valuable education in people's cooking
and shopping habits, making observations that would shape
her ideas and career choices in the near future.

CITY CHALLENGES

Rachael loved the job at Agata & Valentina, but in 1995
something happened that dramatically changed her feelings
about living as a single woman alone in New York City. One
night after working late, as she came home to her apartment
in Queens, two teenage boys entered the vestibule of her
apartment building. While Rachael was reaching for her
keys, one of the boys thrust a gun into her back and
demanded money. Fortunately, Rachael had a vial of pepper
spray that her father had given her. She began screaming
and spraying pepper all over the place, scaring off the star-
tled boys.

Even though she escaped that incident safely, it seemed as
if a dark cloud had settled over Rachael. Three days later she
broke her ankle after falling off a chair at work and had to
hobble around on crutches. She was still using the crutches a
few weeks later when one of the muggers returned. This time
the teen managed to drag Rachael into an alley, hitting her

with his gun and injuring her badly enough that she had to go to the hospital.

While she was recuperating, Rachael decided that she'd had enough of living in the city on her own. She later told *Vanity Fair*:

> Nothing much happened. People have a lot worse things in life. But it was like, O.K., I'm not going to wait for strike three. I felt the whole universe was telling me, "You're not supposed to be here right now."

Rachael asked her family to move her things out of her apartment. She had decided to return home to upstate New York where she would be surrounded by family and close friends again.

View of the Queensboro Bridge, which Rachael often crossed while traveling from her apartment in the New York borough of Queens to her job at Agata & Valentina in Manhattan.

THE 30-MINUTE MEAL

Rachael moved into a cabin in Lake Luzerne, New York, not far from her high school. The rent was $575 a month—expensive for her budget at that time—but she had immediately fallen in love with the cozy little house nestled in the beautiful Adirondack mountains.

She quickly found employment again in the food industry, working in restaurants and managing the pub at The Sagamore, a famous resort on Lake George. About a year later, she was recruited to work at Cowan & Lobel, a large gourmet food market in Albany. She was originally hired as the store's food buyer, in charge of helping to decide which foods the market would carry. When the prepared-foods chef quit one day, however, she offered to take over cooking these dishes, which customers bought and carried out to eat later at home.

As had been the case at Agata & Valentina, Rachael's bosses and colleagues at Cowan & Lobel quickly noticed her work ethic and nonstop energy. "She was a workaholic back then," one of her former coworkers reported. "Her first holiday there, I mean the store was just amazing. It had never looked so good, and we'd never had so many cool things for our holiday."

Lake George, also known as "the queen of American lakes," is located in the Adirondack Mountains in upstate New York. It was the site of Fort William Henry, which was featured in James Fennimore Cooper's 1826 novel about the French and Indian War, *The Last of the Mohicans*. By the early 20th century, Lake George had become a popular resort destination.

As Rachael worked, she also continued listening closely to the customers who were purchasing the store's prepared foods and gourmet pantry items. And what she heard—that they had little time to cook, and were also unsure of how to use many of the gourmet items sold by the store—eventually inspired an idea. Maybe Cowan & Lobel could offer cooking classes! Based on what she'd observed, Rachael was convinced that plenty of customers would like to sign up, especially if the sessions revolved around making simple meals with interesting ingredients.

A marketing promotion by Domino's Pizza, which promised to deliver a pizza in just thirty minutes, also inspired Rachael. "If people will wait thirty minutes for a pizza," she reasoned, "they'd take thirty minutes to cook dinner." She explained the idea to her bosses. "We'll sell gift certificates for a cooking class," Rachael suggested. "We'll find a chef, and we'll call [the classes] '30-Minute Meals.'"

The owners of Cowan & Lobel, who'd been looking for ways to boost sales at their store, loved Rachael's idea. The gift certificates for the cooking classes sold briskly, but they couldn't find a local chef who was willing to teach the classes for the fee that was offered. So Rachael's boss, Donna Carnevale, finally turned back to Rachael and asked her to teach the classes herself. When Rachael reminded Donna that she'd never been trained as a chef and wasn't exactly qualified, Donna replied, "Who cares? Your food's good." So after some more persuasion, Rachael finally agreed to the proposition.

Rachael's class, "30 Minute Meals," quickly became a huge hit at the store. She had noticed that the best-selling take-out dishes in the store were pasta and chicken dishes, so she focused on preparing Mediterranean meals that used

Rachael honed her cooking and public presentation skills by teaching cooking classes at Cowan & Lobel in Albany. She also taught cooking classes at a local supermarket chain.

those ingredients. The class was three hours long. During that time she would teach her students six basic recipes with five different versions of each dish so that they could learn thirty 30-minute meals all at once. She also taught her students how to use a variety of gourmet food items and offered dozens of tips. Some of her favorites include using a "garbage bowl" to collect scraps while cooking, to avoid having to cross the kitchen several times just to reach the garbage can; measuring ingredients more quickly by "eyeballing" the amount; and chopping vegetables more safely and efficiently by cutting off one of the rounded sides to give them flat "legs" to rest on.

The classes at Cowan & Lobel had an instant following. "We had everyone from Girl Scouts and people getting married, to football players and retirees," Rachael later remembered. "It became this Wednesday night thing."

ON TV

Rachael's classes were so popular, they began to attract media attention. Soon the producers of a local news program on the station WRGB in Albany offered Rachael the opportunity to do a cooking segment on TV. Her segment was called "The 30-Minute Meal with Rachael Ray," and it appeared for three minutes once a week. On the show, Rachael often went into people's homes to cook meals with them. As her mother said, "it made for a really cute show

The historic Sagamore resort in the Adirondacks was built in 1883. It was once a social gathering spot for the wealthy who lived along Lake George's "Millionaire Row."

because every [episode] was different." To many it seemed that Rachael was a complete natural, as if she'd always been on TV. Television professionals liked her work as much as audiences did. The first year that the show aired, it was nominated for two regional Emmy awards.

With the help of a producer at WRGB, Rachael also developed a new segment called "Home and Away." Its focus was making travel fun and affordable. Rachael and the producer hoped other TV stations around the country would like the idea and agree to air the segments. This would help to boost Rachael's income and introduce her to a wider audience. Unfortunately, "Home and Away" enjoyed only moderate success, and no other TV stations expressed interest in broadcasting it.

Rachael liked the work she was doing, but in late 1997 she left her job at Cowan & Lobel. Her boss and friend Donna Carnevale had been forced out of her job as manager due to a family dispute, and Rachael decided she did not want

Rachael's original idea for a television show on eating and travel, "Home and Away," did not immediately take off during her time working with Albany television station WRGB. She would later refine the idea to create the successful Food Network series $40 a Day.

to continue working at the gourmet market. "Rachael said, 'If I don't work for you, I'm not going to work here,'" Donna later told *Vanity Fair*. "She's extremely loyal—beyond. Loyalty to a fault. She had no job lined up. Nothing. She just left."

Rachael soon found work with the Price Chopper supermarket chain, which operated stores in western and central New York state. She would travel from store to store, demonstrating how to cook 30-minute meals on a small two-burner stove atop a folding table. Between this job and filming the TV segments, she was constantly busy. But there were months when Rachael could barely pay the rent on the cabin she shared with her mom and her dog, a pit bull named Boo. The TV segments paid only about $50 per episode, and the Price Chopper job paid little more. "It was check-to-check living," she later recalled. The constant struggle to make ends meet was getting to be a problem. Luckily, Rachael was about to get two big breaks.

Rachael signs copies of one of her cookbooks in a New York bookstore. The surprise success of her first cookbook, 30-Minute Meals, helped launch Rachael to fame in 2001.

CHAPTER FOUR

The New Celebrity Chef

By 1998 Rachael had collected hundreds of "30-Minute" recipes. She also had a stack of treasured recipes left behind by her grandfather, Emmanuel Scudieri, who'd passed away. "People started writing me angry mail that they couldn't get the recipes, and they couldn't keep track of them," Rachael explained in *Newsweek* magazine. So she decided it was time to try to publish her "30-Minute Meal" recipes in a book.

A Surprising Bestseller

That summer Rachael contacted Lake Isle Press, a small publisher in New York City. At first the company wasn't at all interested in an unknown author with a stash of 30-minute recipes. In fact, the idea of recipes that could be prepared in thirty minutes wasn't completely new. There were many other cookbooks available then with a similar focus—preparing meals in just minutes.

After meeting Rachael in person, however, Lake Isle Press publisher Hiroko Kiiffner changed her mind. Rachael's dynamic personality impressed Kiiffner, and so did Rachael's persistence. In addition, the Price Chopper grocery store chain had promised to carry Rachael's cookbook in its upstate New York stores. So Kiiffner agreed to publish Rachael's book.

As soon as they had a deal, Rachael boldly asked for something else: Could the book be published very quickly—in time for that year's holiday selling season? Kiifner later described her astonished reaction. "That's impossible!" she told Rachael. "We just don't work that way."

But once again, Rachael was very persuasive—and three months later, her very first cookbook was released. *30-Minute Meals* featured simple meals with easy-to-follow directions and helpful planning lists such as Top 10 Meals, Top 10 Meals with Fewer Than 10 Ingredients, and Top 10 Kids' Favorites, which included Mini-Meatball Soup, Zesty Chicken Cutlets Parmigiana, and other kid-friendly foods. Many of the tips that Rachael had been teaching in her cooking classes also appeared, for example: "Change recipes to reflect your own tastes," the sound of the garlic sizzling "is the sound of the garlic telling you to add more stuff to the pan now," and "whenever you use a knife, shake hands with the handle."

Rachael dedicated this first book to her mother. "You taught me that living the good life is as simple as eating good food," she wrote, "and that peace is found in the smiles of our loved ones (so stay close to home)."

To the surprise of many, *30-Minute Meals* was an instant hit. In just two weeks, the first printing of ten thousand copies was sold out—an amazing feat for a first-time author. The book was reprinted quickly. For Rachael, the cookbook's publication—and receiving the payment for it—

marked her first major professional success. She later recalled the moment:

> My mom and I got the check . . . and we danced through the streets and just thought it was the most money in the world ever. We went to a really great restaurant and bought nice dresses for ourselves and had the best time.

This was an important turning point in Rachael's career. Now she was not only a teacher and a cook; she was a published author with a highly successful book.

TWO BIG BREAKS

That first cookbook, along with Rachael's short segments on WRGB, helped her gain some local fame in the Albany area. In 2001, though, she had two big breaks that would put her in the national spotlight, where she could finally be seen by millions of viewers across the country.

The first big break came when the *Today* show called, inviting her to be a guest during that big blizzard that was threatened in March. The second break arrived via the Food Network, which contacted Rachael around the same time.

The Food Network, now a very successful cable network, had launched about eight years earlier with cooking shows that were both entertaining and informational. Some of the network's first star chefs included Emeril Lagasse, Bobby Flay, and Mario Batali. Many people believed that the Food Network's success was due to very smart—or very fortunate—timing. It had begun producing shows about food at a time when Americans were growing more interested in cooking with gourmet and imported foods, and when these foods were becoming more readily available in local grocery stores rather than only in specialty markets. *The New York Times* declared that the Food Network's "knack for spotting hosts who could appeal to viewers while pan-searing a chicken breast made it a ratings powerhouse." After all, a chef has to have quite a personality to make something as ordinary as cooking a chicken breast look like fun!

In 2001, a man named Lou Ekus heard Rachael on the radio in upstate New York. She was cooking a 30-minute jambalaya, and Ekus was impressed with her bubbly person-ality and very accessible approach to what could be a compli-cated recipe. As it turned out, Ekus knew the senior vice president of programming at the Food Network. When Ekus told his friend about Rachael, saying that she'd been very entertaining—especially for a radio appearance—Bob Tuschman was instantly intrigued. He set up a meeting with Rachael, even though he was still unsure if she would be right for the Food Network. For one thing, the hosts on that net-work were professionally trained chefs who had graduated from prestigious cooking schools such as the Culinary Institute of America. Rachael, on the other hand, had learned to cook from her mother and grandfather, at home in her family's kitchen. Without having seen Rachael in person, Tuschman also did not know if she would be appealing on TV.

When Tuschman heard that Rachael was going to appear on *Today*, he tuned in to watch. What he saw left a deep impres-sion. "I watched her on the *Today* show and she was astound-ing," he later said. "She grabbed the camera, she lit up the screen, she was fun, not polished, but fun." He was hooked.

ON THE FOOD NETWORK

The day after Rachael appeared on the *Today* show, she met with Bob Tuschman and other executives at the New York

THE CULINARY INSTITUTE OF AMERICA

The Culinary Institute of America is one of the best cooking schools in the United States. It was founded in 1946 and has its main campus in Hyde Park, New York. To enroll at the Culinary Institute, students must have worked at least six months in the food service industry. The program also requires outside work experience of eighteen months at an approved food-service facility. Culinary Institute students can earn degrees in culinary arts or in baking and pastry arts. The classes are taught by some of the most famous and respected chefs in the world. Home cooks can also take classes there for fun, without earning a degree.

The Culinary Institute has five restaurants that are open to the public in Hyde Park. Students work in the restaurants' kitchens and also out front, interacting with other staff members and restaurant patrons to gain management skills. Some famous graduates of the Culinary Institute of America include chefs Anthony Bourdain, Cat Cora, Sara Moulton, and Todd English.

The Hyde Park, New York, campus of the Culinary Institute of America.

City offices of the Food Network. Rachel told the network execs that she felt out of her depth. The national network was loaded with culinary superstars, while she had no formal training as a chef. "I said, 'Listen, you're champagne, I'm beer out of the bottle. I clearly don't belong here, I'm not a chef, you've been duped,'" Rachael later recalled. "And I got up. And they said, "No, no, no, stop. That's what we like. We don't want you to be a chef."

It was Rachael's turn to be surprised. The Food Network was still interested in her, even without any professional training? In fact, that's precisely what they found so appealing about her. She was down-to-earth, with a funny and relaxed style of cooking that was refreshing and new. The Food Network executives had a feeling that many Americans would relate to her and enjoy watching her cook on TV. According to Brooke Johnson, the president of the Food Network:

> Rachael came along with the right idea at the right time. Cooking used to be hours and hours in the kitchen, and obviously, with the number of working women in this country, they don't have time to do it. Rachael figured that out and gave it a great name; really fun, interesting ingredients; ways to mix and match—just things you wouldn't think of.

Rachael chooses to dress like a regular home cook. Professionally trained chefs, on the other hand, usually wear white jackets to signify their role in the kitchen— and to stay cool when it gets hot in there! The traditional long sleeves of a chef's uniform also protect his or her arms from burns.

Johnson also attributed Rachael's appeal to her personality. "She's got a big, big personality," she said. "She doesn't hide from you, and that's very attractive to people. She has vulnerability because she's so open. . . . And she has tremendous energy. She jumps off the screen."

That day, because of Rachael's big personality and her very marketable 30-minute meals concept, the Food Network gave her a contract to create not one, but two shows. She would shoot 25 episodes of *30-Minute Meals* and 40 episodes of *$40 a Day*, a travel show for people on a low budget. The contract was for $360,000. After years of struggling to make ends meet, this was a tremendous amount of money for Rachael. The first thing she used it for was reupholstering all the old furniture in her cabin in upstate New York. Then she bought the cabin itself, that special place that she had considered home for such a long time.

Rachael was amazed by everything that was happening to her. But in a way it wasn't surprising, as Laura Jacobs wrote in *Vanity Fair*:

> What's interesting is that she'd actually envisioned this path. Her mom remembers that late one night, helping put the final touches on the first cookbook, she asked Rachael, "If this ever became anything, where do you see yourself in five years?" Ray answered, "I would love to be on *The Oprah Winfrey Show* or I'd love to work for the Food Network."

LIGHTS, CAMERA, ACTION!

The Food Network aired the first episode of *30-Minute Meals* on November 2, 2001. Rachael was nervous during the taping, which showed in her slightly subdued manner. This was very unusual for Rachael, who is often called

Rachael prepares soup on an early episode of her Food Network TV show 30-Minute Meals. From the start, the show was a major hit for the network.

"perky" and "bubbly." She was also completely unaccustomed to having so much help in the kitchen. One day she poured olive oil into a pan without realizing that an assistant had preheated the pan for her, so it burst into flames. Rachael herself was near tears, worried that she wasn't ready for national TV after all.

True to her personality, though, Rachael worked very hard to make the show a success. And she never altered her personality for her new wider audience, as *Success* magazine reported:

> Ray leapt into television . . . heeding the words of her mother and mentor . . . "You must strive to get wherever it is you want to go, but remember that you can't be all things to all people. So decide who and what you are and don't try to pretend that you're something other than that."

30-Minute Meals quickly became one of the network's most popular programs, mainly because of what the Food Network executives had seen—Rachael's big, appealing personality and her smart idea, born years before at Cowan & Lobel, to make cooking simple and accessible to untrained people. Bob Tuschman said she instantly

Today some of the biggest stars at the Food Network include Nigella Lawson, Mario Batali, Guy Fieri, Paula Deen, Alton Brown, Cat Cora, and Giada De Laurentiis. Each of these chefs has their own unique cooking style and certain types of dishes that they are best known for, from Paula Deen's traditional Southern cooking to De Laurentiis' Italian cuisine.

Other cable channels began developing more cooking shows after the success of the Food Network, including programs like *Top Chef* and *Rocco's Dinner Party* on Bravo and *Cake Boss* and *DC Cupcakes* on TLC.

"electrified audiences" because of her accessible way of speaking directly to home cooks.

It was still true, however, that Rachael had never been trained professionally, unlike all the other chefs on the Food Network. She didn't know classic methods for chopping onions and preparing sauces. To the horror of many people, she often suggested shortcuts to viewers, such as using ready-made ingredients for her recipes—boxed cake mix, canned chicken broth, salad bags, and packages of shredded cheese or precut frozen vegetables. Other chefs would prepare such ingredients from scratch, but Rachael understood that most home cooks do not have the time to do this. She also told viewers they didn't have to measure precisely; instead they could just "eyeball" mixtures, toss in "half a palm-full" of something, or add "two glugs," Rachael's word for small portions of wine. That lack of precision might mortify a classically trained chef, but it helped ordinary home cooks feel more comfortable trying their hand at new recipes. As Food Network president Brooke Johnson pointed out in a *Good Housekeeping* article, Rachael's special gift lay in skills she'd developed as a child and honed as a cooking teacher: She was good at "canoodling" recipes, simplifying them and paring them down so that dishes could be prepared by anyone in thirty minutes or less. As Johnson said, "She is a world-class recipe developer."

$40 A DAY

By the end of 2001, Rachael had published another cookbook, *Veggie Meals: Rachael Ray's 30-Minute Meals*, which focused on vegetarian dishes. She was also very busy working on the travel show *$40 a Day*, which debuted in 2002. Rachael's job on the show was to explore primarily American or European cities, finding fun things to do and good places to eat—restaurants, picnic locations, ice creams stands, and so on—while spending no more than $40 a day.

Unlike the *30-Minute Meals* show, *$40 a Day* was not an instant success. Over time, though, its popularity grew. Rachael enjoyed filming the program because she had not been able to afford much travel in the past. Now the show was opening doors, giving her the chance to see many new parts of the world as she showed viewers how they could eat cheaply in Rome, spend the holidays in New York City, drink smoothies in Antigua, or eat a Cuban sandwich in South Beach, Florida.

Rachael had become a bright light at the Food Network, a quickly rising star who had easily attracted millions of fans. That stardom came with a price, though. It put the spotlight on her lack of professional training, and that brought plenty of criticism her way as well.

As she became the most popular Food Network personality, Rachael found herself in constant demand from the media.

CHAPTER FIVE

FAME AND FORTUNE

By 2002, just a year after the debut of *30-Minute Meals* on the Food Network, Rachael had become a household name. Her TV presence also helped to boost sales of her first cookbook, *30-Minute Meals*. That year it made it onto *USA Today*'s list of bestselling books.

Despite her growing fame, Rachael seemed to stay balanced. She credits her mother with helping her deal with success. "I was raised with a decent work ethic and more importantly a great sense of humor," Rachael shared in an interview with *Redbook* magazine. "As long as you've got a good work ethic and a sense of humor, I don't think anybody can become too much of an egoist under those circumstances."

Her goofy personality didn't change either, even as she gained hundreds of hours of national TV experience. A birthday celebration at the Food Network during Rachael's first year there provides a good example. "I was taping, and they brought me out this big cake and I leaned in," she laughed.

"I set both sides of my hair on fire. At the same time. With my own birthday candles. I am a train wreck."

RACHAEL'S CRITICS

Unfortunately, the very things that seemed to make Rachael popular with most viewers tended to annoy some people, especially other celebrity cooks. Some media reviewers, and even a few of the other chefs at the Food Network, criticized her lack of classical training and the way she built shortcuts into her recipes. Rachael's critics also deplored her failure to measure ingredients properly and her constant clumsiness as fruit rolled across her sets, ingredients spilled, and she burnt or cut herself.

Actress Kristin Davis gets a cooking lesson from Rachael and her fellow Food Network star Mario Batali on the Rachael Ray *show. When some people— including some chefs—criticized Rachael's style or lack of formal training, Batali came to her defense.*

Another Food Network chef, Mario Batali—who later became a good friend of Rachael's—speculated that some of the criticism stemmed from jealousy, especially because her cookbooks were so successful. As he pointed out:

> She single-handedly changed the entire cookbook market, and a lot of chefs aren't happy about that. Someone sells 50,000 copies of a book, it used to be considered very nice. Rachael's upped the ante.

A very vocal group of Rachael Ray critics emerged online. Several blogs and social networking sites sprang up for the sole purpose of making fun of her and critiquing her shows. According to an article in the *New York Times*, one online group—which had more than one thousand members—was "quite active in posting their latest thoughts and observations about the various shortcomings, flaws, and disagreeable traits of Rachael Ray, the television personality."

Like several of the professional chefs who were criticizing Rachael, the people posting on these sites attacked her use of cooking shortcuts and her lack of classical training. They also ridiculed the way she talked, her constant use of cutesy catchphrases such as "delish," "eyeball it," "sammies" (for sandwiches), and "EVOO" (for extra-virgin olive oil). The internet critics homed in on very personal things, too—her hair, weight, and style of dress.

A WRITER COMES TO RACHAEL'S DEFENSE

Jill Hunter Pellettieri of *Slate* magazine observed that Rachael's critics seemed particularly annoyed by Rachael's habit of gushing over her own food. "They can't stand the way she responds to her own cooking," Pellettieri commented. "She's so enthusiastic." Pellettieri wrote an article entitled

"Rachael Ray: Why Food Snobs Should Quit Picking on Her," which was a defense of Rachael's talents and her *30-Minute Meals* show:

> The show is fantastically entertaining . . . and . . . suspenseful. As the minutes tick by, Ray becomes frenetic—will she finish? (She always does.) And it's educational. As Ray trims her asparagus . . . she offers tips. Use a "garbage bowl" to collect debris as you're cooking. . . . Roll citrus before you cut it, and you'll extract more juice.

To the delight of many critics, though, Pellettieri went on to admit that she had tried Rachael's recipes—and was unable to complete a single one of them in under thirty minutes:

> As [Rachael] became more popular and her detractors became more vocal, I realized that if I wanted to defend her, I should try a few of her recipes. You can imagine my dismay when, 21 recipes later, I was forced to admit that I could not complete a 30-Minute Meal in 30 minutes.

Nevertheless, in the end, Pellettieri came full circle in her admiration for Rachael's work:

> Her Super Sloppy Joes certainly aren't haute cuisine, but that's no reason for highfalutin' chefs to knock her. Consider what Ray brings to the table: Creativity, adeptness, speed. Her skills are as estimable as those of any Michelin-star-winning chef, and they're far more practical. . . . I'm still making "30-Minute Meals." And you know what? They do smell awesome.

RACHAEL-ISMS

Here are some of Rachael's favorite food or cooking terms, often called "Rachael-isms:"

EVOO: extra-virgin olive oil

eyeball it: estimate an amount by sight instead of measuring it precisely

GH: "grown-up helper" in charge of things such as boiling water or handling heavy cookware in Rachael's recipes for kids

jambalika: a dish like jambalaya, which is a Cajun stew

sammie: a sandwich

stoup: a very thick soup that is more like a stew

two turns: to go twice around the inside of the pan with oil

yum-o!: very tasty or delicious

motz: short for "mozzarella cheese"

As for her part, Rachael handled her critics in an unusual way—mainly by agreeing with them. "Most of what they say is absolutely true," she told *Vanity Fair*. "I don't know how to bake. I didn't make my own pierogies in episode whatever. You can't be all things to all people." Regarding the websites that were created to mock her, she tries her best to just shrug off the criticism. "What am I going to do?" she commented in *Good Housekeeping*. "Call them up and scream, 'You have to like me'? It's like trying to get the class bully to be your buddy—a waste of time."

Michelin ratings are a popular way for customers to find out about high-quality restaurants. One star is awarded for "very good" food, while the highest rating of three stars is considered outstanding or exceptional.

HARD WORK

Rachael's schedule at the Food Network continued to be very demanding. She had to travel frequently for *$40 a Day* in addition to filming *30-Minute Meals* in New York City, developing new recipes, writing more cookbooks, and making media appearances around the country. Though life was hectic, that fast pace suited Rachael, who had never shied away from hard work or a packed schedule. "I can't really sit idle," she commented in *Redbook*. "I don't mind if it's a rainy day watching TV all day in bed with my dog. That's fun. But generally speaking . . . it freaks me out to . . . be still. . . . I work a lot. I always have."

"I don't think Rachael Ray sleeps," agreed CBS-TV executive Terry Wood. "That's my theory. . . . I'm pretty sure I'm right about this." Doralece Dullaghan, the director of promotions for the company that sells Rachael's line of cookware, echoed that sentiment in the *New York Times*: "She's a machine. . . . I think she's one of those for-the-moment people who never stops working."

But Rachael's mother expressed worry about Rachael's pace. "She and I have words about it often," she said. "I think that Rachael needs time to rest. We all need time to rest."

Rachael, however, showed no sign of slowing down. Still, she did have some time left over for fun. She'd met an entertainment lawyer and musician named John Cusimano in

2001. They were introduced at a party, an encounter they'd both later call "love at first sight." In a CNN interview, John described his side of that story to Larry King: "My very good friend who was with me and single at the time looked at me and goes, 'oh, you are done.'"

Like Rachael, John loved food, and he was also a musician, the lead singer and guitarist for a punk rock band, The Cringe. With both music and food in common, the two spent a lot of their free time together.

Rachael Ray and John Cusimano attend an event in Washington, D.C.

Rachael loves to see kids cooking in the kitchen. She believes that cooking is creative, boosts kids' self-esteem, and teaches math skills. Here she works with a young cook on an episode of her Food Network show 30 Minute Meals.

A COOKBOOK FOR KIDS

In the meantime, Rachael's cookbook industry was growing. She continued publishing cookbooks, all spinoffs of her 30-minute meals idea. After the first two—*30-Minute Meals* and *30-Minute Veggie Meals*—came *30-Minute Meals 2* and *30-Minute Comfort Meals.*

Rachael always had a special interest in teaching kids how to cook and how to eat nutritiously. So she aimed one of her new cookbooks specifically at children. Published in 2004, *Cooking Rocks! Rachael Ray 30-Minute Meals for Kids* included more than one hundred recipes for kids aged four to sixteen. Some of the dishes had special "secret" ingredients and funny names that were high in kid appeal, such as Crunchy Oven-Baked Chicken Toes, Birds in a Nest with Blankets, and Cookie and Ice Cream Fill-Your-Handwiches. The book also featured lots of helpful hints for children learning how to cook, including such tips as "clean pots and dishes as you cook so you don't have a ton of cleanup afterwards," and "small heavy skillets are handy for other things beyond frying. . . . You can use them to pound chicken cutlets to make them thinner or to squish garlic." There was also a special section on how to handle knives (very carefully). Rachael dedicated this cookbook "to cool kids everywhere who love to eat and cook!"

By now Rachael was producing a lot of cookbooks, but she had some guiding principles, or rules, that applied to all of them. One was that the price of her books had to be kept low, as she explained in *Vanity Fair*:

> I won't allow the books to be pricier than a music CD. Because they're collections of everything that I do on-air, and I just feel you shouldn't be paying more than you would for a popular song. I consider my food the equivalent of a pop song.

Her other principles also kept the readers' needs front and center:

> The recipes can't require special tools. . . . I always try to pay attention to what my readers say they want more of from my previous books. I never put anything in the books that I haven't come up with myself. And I try everything too, since I am not a chef.

When Rachael published *30-Minute Meals 2*, John accompanied her on the book tour. He soon noticed that her fans frequently asked her what kinds of products she used in the kitchen, such as knives and dishes and pantry items. That observation inspired Rachael to develop her own line of kitchen products. The Rachael Ray brand included knives, food processors, and colorful pans and pots, including a special oval-shaped pot that she invented just for cooking long sticks of spaghetti. She also developed her own brand of olive oil, called "EVOO," of course!

A MULTIMILLION DOLLAR CONTRACT

Eventually Rachael signed with the William Morris Agency, a well-known talent agency for writers and entertainers. Rachael's new agent persuaded her that it was time to leave the Lake Isle Press publishing company and move to Clarkson Potter, a much bigger cookbook publisher. Clarkson Potter not only wanted to produce new cookbooks with Rachael; they also were interested in acquiring the rights to all of Rachael's earlier books. Now they were offering her a $6 million contract.

Rachael knew this offer represented a wonderful opportunity, both financially and for her career in general. But she felt a great deal of loyalty toward Lake Isle Press and Hiroko Kiiffner, who had taken a chance on Rachael when she was virtually unknown. Eventually they worked out a deal in which Lake Isle Press could continue publishing any of the

Rachael's husband John, a musician, wrote a song for her when they were dating, called "Burn." It was the first song released from The Cringe's first album, *Scratch the Surface* (2005).

books they had done with Rachael. Kiiffner described Rachael's move to Clarkson Potter as painful, but still the publisher appreciated Rachael's loyalty. "Rachael has a long memory for those who helped her get started," Kiiffner told *Good Housekeeping*. "We'll always be a part of each other's lives because of our shared history. We're still good friends."

THE FHM CONTROVERSY

In 2003 Rachael became the focus of a minor controversy when the men's magazine *FHM* contacted the Food Network to ask if Rachael might be interested in doing a photo shoot for *FHM*. Some of the photos would feature Rachael wearing very short shorts and a shirt that showed her midriff as she licked chocolate off a big spoon. In another photo, she'd be wearing a black bra and a short frilly apron as she took a turkey out of the oven. After talking over the opportunity with John, Rachael decided that it would be fun and decided to go ahead. She believed it was a positive message compared with the unrealistic body image often perpetuated by the photos of super-skinny models that normally appear in such magazines. "I thought if I'm gutsy enough to do this, this is a good thing for everybody," she later explained to *Nightline* anchorwoman Cynthia McFadden. "This is the everywoman, here she is."

Rachael's mother was furious with her daughter, though, and very critical of this decision. Elsa felt that posing for these pictures was offensive to Rachael and to all women. She wasn't the only one who didn't approve. For the websites devoted to making fun of Rachael—and for chefs who already looked down on her lack of professional training—the photo shoot represented more proof of what they considered her unprofessionalism. It quickly became another opportunity to ridicule her.

Rachael and John asked their wedding guests to contribute to animal rescue charities instead of giving them a gift.

Still, Rachael has said that she didn't regret her choice. "It was the most scared I've ever been and I wouldn't change a thing. I'd do it again tomorrow."

A WEDDING IN TUSCANY

In the meantime, Rachael's personal life continued to move along. In 2005, after several years of dating, Rachael and John decided to get married. For Rachael—who was still juggling many professional demands, from developing recipes for her cookbooks to filming TV shows—John was the ideal mate. "I can't give a man an enormous amount of attention," she explained to *People* magazine. "And John is totally down with that. When men I have dated over the years whined about, 'Oh, you make no time for me,' . . . I just dumped them. I don't need that pressure in my life."

The couple got married on September 24 in Montalcino, a town in the Tuscany region of Italy. It was a location that had become a favorite of Rachael's during her travels. The wedding—planned mainly by her mother, her mother's best friend, and John—was held in a castle. Rachael paid for more than a hundred guests to fly to Italy for the occasion. Afterward the couple went to Aspen, Colorado, for their honeymoon. And Rachael, who had never had an easy time sitting still or relaxing, actually spent part of her honeymoon working—on another cookbook, of course!

CHAPTER SIX

A GROWING EMPIRE

By 2005 Rachael had become the most popular host on the Food Network. She was on the air for thirteen hours each week, with more than 18 million people watching her during those hours. In addition to the original two shows that Rachael had developed, the Food Network was now offering her a chance to host two more programs, *Tasty Travels* and *Inside Dish*.

Tasty Travels was another travel-oriented show that featured Rachael tracking down good food and other culinary "secrets" on the road. In one episode, she sampled tropical treats on the island of Trinidad. In others, she revealed the best restaurants in Austin, Texas, or looked for oysters at 2 A.M. in Boston. Unlike its companion program *$40 a Day*, *Tasty Travels* did not focus solely on low-budget destinations and activities. And just like *30-Minute Meals*, the new travel show was an instant success. When it debuted in August of 2005 its ratings were the second highest of any other premiere on the Food Network, exceeded only by *Iron Chef America*.

Rachael's other new show, *Inside Dish*, did not involve travel. Instead, it featured Rachael cooking with celebrities at their homes or in restaurants that they owned in order to give viewers an "inside look" at how the rich and famous cook and eat. In some of the early episodes of *Inside Dish*, Rachael ate lunch with NYPD Blue actor Dennis Franz at his home, dined at the Mississippi restaurant owned by movie star Morgan Freeman, and helped actress/singer Raven-Symoné prepare baked ziti.

That year Rachael also published two more cookbooks, *Rachael Ray's 365: No Repeats—A Year of Deliciously Different Dinners* and *Rachael Ray's 30-Minute Get Real Meals: Eat Healthy Without Going to Extremes*. The first one, *Rachael Ray's 365*, had been especially difficult to produce because it provided a new recipe for every day of the year—365 in all, of course. As Rachael joked later in the *New York Times*, "That was the stupidest idea I ever had. That many recipes nearly killed me."

EVERY DAY WITH RACHAEL RAY

Rachael began working on another ambitious new project in 2005 as well, a food and lifestyle magazine called *Every Day with Rachael Ray*. As the magazine's editor-in-chief, she had a very specific vision for the magazine right from the start. She insisted that her new magazine feature articles that

Rachael offers many tips to help busy home cooks. One of her key tips is to keep the pantry stocked with the "building blocks" of fast meals: rice, pasta, broths, canned beans, canned tomatoes, and (of course) extra-virgin olive oil.

Rachael proudly shows off a copy of the first issue of her magazine, Every Day with Rachael Ray, *October 2005. By 2012,* Every Day with Rachael Ray *had a circulation of 1.7 million, making it another important piece of Rachael's growing media empire.*

would appeal to everyday people, the home cooks and working mothers who had always been her core fans. "I want to see legitimately useful information: here are shoes you can cook in and party in," she explained in the *New York Times.* "This is more about customer service. . . . I grew up working in resort-town restaurants. In my mind I'm a waitress. I want to give the people what they want."

Shortly before *Every Day with Rachael Ray* was scheduled to go on sale, newsstands and stores had already ordered

MEASURING INGREDIENTS A LA RACHAEL

"Cooking is loose—a little of this, a little of that."
—From *Kid Food: Rachael Ray's Top 30 30-Minute Meals* (New York: Lake Isle Press), 2005.

"a pinch"= about 1/4 teaspoon

"a few good pinches" = about 1 teaspoon

"once around the pan" = about 1 tablespoon

"twice around the pan" = about 2 tablespoons

"a palmful" = about 2 tablespoons

"a handful" = about 3 tablespoons

more than 800,000 copies. That was a huge number for any magazine, especially a brand-new one. From the start it was obvious that Rachael had another huge success on her hands.

BOO AND ISABOO

The year 2005 also brought a heartbreaking loss when Rachael's beloved dog, Boo, died. Boo was a pit bull that Rachel had adopted when a family could no longer care for her. Rachael explained in the magazine *Vegetarian Star* how Boo had come into her life:

> The dog was so high energy—[the family was] just worried they wouldn't be able to spend the kind of time with [her] that they should. They didn't want a

Rachael hugs her pit bull, Isaboo. She has been outspoken in her support for this breed, despite the reputation of pit bulls as dangerous dogs. Over the years Rachael has donated generously to rescue organizations dedicated to helping abandoned animals.

penny; . . . they just wanted to make sure she went to the right person. She was with me through . . . half a dozen boyfriends, a couple of jobs, and two muggings. I got her in my early 20s, and I had her for 13 years.

Rachael was devastated by the loss of her longtime pet. A few months later, though, she and John decided they were ready to adopt another dog. "Isaboo" was a pit bull, just like Boo. Rachael was committed to adopting more of this breed, which she believed was often misunderstood by the public. "They're some of the sweetest animals on earth," she commented to CNN's Larry King. "Boo was afraid of her own voice. If she would bark too loud, she'd run and hide under the sofa and I'd have to coax her out with treats."

DAYTIME TV

Meanwhile, Rachael's fan base continued to grow, and the executives at the Food Network weren't the only ones to notice Rachael's widespread appeal. One night CBS-TV executive Terry Wood saw her seven-year-old daughter glued to the television:

> I came home from work, and [my daughter] was watching Rachael on television. She could name all her shows. I said, "Why do you like her?" She said, "I just like right here," and she was pointing to the frame of her face. I thought, if she can drag a seven-year-old to the set, the possibilities must be endless.

Soon Wood called the Food Network, and the two networks began discussing the possibility of working together to produce a new show starring Rachael. By then, Oprah Winfrey—whose own daytime television show had been on the air for years—had also noticed Rachael's remarkable gift as a TV personality. "In order to do a television show," Winfrey explained in *Time* magazine, "the most important quality a host needs to have is the ability to be themselves day after day—on camera. And that's what [Rachael] has."

Winfrey believed that the time was right for Rachael to launch her own syndicated daytime talk show. A syndicated show is not restricted to one network only, but can be broadcast on multiple channels. Soon plans were underway for the new daytime show to be distributed by King World

Rachael chats with legendary talk show host and entrepreneur Oprah Winfrey during one of the first episodes of her daytime program Rachael Ray. *Oprah helped launch the show in September 2006, and it became an immediate hit for CBS.*

Productions in partnership with Harpo, Oprah Winfrey's production company.

Just as with the launch of her magazine, Rachael had some very specific ideas about what her daytime show should be like. She wanted the tone to be upbeat. "Everything in the show [will have] a sense of humor," she told *Redbook* magazine. "We're gonna do a lot. . . . I love giving entertaining advice and how to throw parties, and gift-giving advice, that kind of thing."

Rachael was also determined to center the new show on regular people rather than celebrities. "We want the normal people to feel like celebs," she said in *USA Today*. Rachael wanted the set to feel intimate and friendly, as if viewers were just dropping into a neighbor's kitchen for a cup of coffee. She also hoped that the audience would be a big part of the action. With all of this in mind, the set was designed with a rustic Mediterranean look, featuring exposed brick walls and other details that would make it feel casual and homey. It was built around the audience, with the viewers' seats attached to a platform that could be rotated to face Rachael wherever she happened to be on the set. Rachael expanded on this idea on CNN:

> There's a lot of viewer involvement and accessibility is the key. The number one goal of everything I do or am involved in [is] can people watch it and picture themselves doing it, trying it, living it easily. . . . Hopefully we'll make them laugh and . . . have a lot of good food.

ON THE AIR

The first episode of the daytime show *Rachael Ray* aired on September 18, 2006. Even before its premiere it was a huge attraction, with a waiting list of more than 19,000 names for the 115 seats. One fan, a stay-at-home mom, explained why she wanted to see Rachael's show in person: "She's like everybody. She doesn't think she's better than everyone else. . . . And she doesn't mind being corny."

According to a *Broadcasting & Cable* report, the first episode "debuted with . . . the best talk show launch numbers in four years and second best in the past decade." It finished fourth, behind three already well-established and successful shows—*Oprah*, *Dr. Phil*, and *Live with Regis & Kelly*. On the night of the show's debut, Larry King asked Rachael if she'd been nervous at the taping of the first show. Her response showed that she was still the same Rachael as always:

> I was so nervous; I thought it was good luck though . . . on the Food Network I was talking with my hands and I cut this finger off on my first day. [On] the show that aired today, our very first show of *Rachael Ray Show* I cut into the cuticle of this finger.

Once again many Americans seemed to delight in Rachael's casual, down-to-earth, and often klutzy presence. The show also drew praise from the media. *Time* magazine said Rachael's "main attribute was her accessibility" and described how she managed to create that atmosphere: "During the daily snack time on her talk show, she walks out and personally serves her audience food, and unlike many TV

Rachael has described her 2001 appearance on *Sesame Street* as one of her favorite TV moments. Her job was to present the word of the day: "pumpernickel," a dark sourdough bread.

hosts, she makes it feel as though she's chatting instead of lecturing. She is the most accessible celebrity ever."

Rachael also made sure that kids were a big part of the show, as she told *Redbook*:

All of our walls here—and our refrigerator—are covered with kids' art, and kids write us their recipes all the time. We have cooking segments here and there, and we go and get kids' opinions on a lot of stuff. I love talking to kids. They're very self-effacing; they have a great sense of humor.

But not everyone was impressed by the new *Rachael Ray* show. Alessandra Stanley, a TV critic for the *New York Times*, slammed the show and described Rachael's personality as "brash" and even irritating:

Ms. Ray's first show was beyond bubbly. Watching it was like opening a shaken bottle of club soda and having it fizz all over the room. On a set meant to look like a cozy, slightly tacky New York apartment (she said she decorated it herself), Ms. Ray casts herself as America's big sister. . . . Ms. Ray has more than four million books in print, four shows in regular rotation on the Food Network, her own food and lifestyle magazine, *Every Day with Rachael Ray*, and Oprah Winfrey as her patron. She seems more like the hyperactive little sister who is compelled always to outshine and outdo her older siblings.

For Rachael's online critics, the new show provided still more opportunities to mock her clothing, her way of cooking, and even her smile. But as *New York Times* reporter Rob Walker pointed out, even though the online communities that disliked

Rachael were growing in numbers, they seemed to "have had no impact on [her popularity] whatsoever." A marketing consultant commented in the same article, "If you've got a fan base . . . you can weather negative word of mouth."

A VERY BIG YEAR

After the launch of the *Rachael Ray* show, Rachael's popularity continued to increase. By October of 2006, *30-Minute Meals* was the highest rated show on the Food Network, and the audience for *$40 a Day* was growing as well. According to a *New York Times* article, the *Every Day with Rachael Ray* magazine was "exploding, with a promised circulation of 1.7 million by next year. As an author, Ms. Ray has few peers with sixteen cookbooks that have a total sales of nearly five million."

In 2006 Rachael also agreed to become the spokesperson for the food company Nabisco, and that year *Forbes* magazine named her the "second most trusted celebrity" while *Business Week* honored her as one of the "Best Leaders of 2006." Then *Time* magazine included her as number 81 on its list of "100 Most Influential People." Rachael was stunned by her inclusion on *Time*'s list. For her it was a huge honor to be included among this elite group of leaders, especially since she still saw herself as a "burger flipper." As she said on Biography.com, "I just showed [people] how to make some easy restaurant food. . . . I found it ridiculous that I made that list. . . . It was a jaw-dropping, once-in-a-lifetime experience." She also joked about feeling out of place at the celebratory dinner held for the people on the list. "I felt like I was going to trip on my dress and do something really stupid . . . somehow knock the water over the table all over the president of so and so or the Nobel Prize winner over there."

Time's profile of Rachael, however—which was written by chef Mario Batali in honor of the occasion—captured the contributions that Rachael had made to the world of cooking in such a short time:

> In fewer than five years, Rachael Ray . . . has radically changed the way America cooks dinner. Her perky-girl-next-door swagger, her catchphrases for techniques and her dinner ideology of simpler, less expensive and just in time have sold billions of books and placed her at the top of . . . the Food Network. . . . Her ease with basic kitchen techniques and a simple-to-find-in-Topeka ingredient list does not challenge viewers but entices them to join her.

When Rachael read what her colleague had written about her, she was so moved that she burst into tears.

CHAPTER SEVEN

GIVING BACK

In 2006—already a big year for Rachael—she enjoyed another exciting TV victory. This one came on the set of *Iron Chef America*, a show that the Food Network had modeled after *Iron Chef*, a hit Japanese cooking show that featured cooks battling one another in dramatic cooking competitions. The American version kept the basic premise, with two chefs teaming up to challenge another pair in the "kitchen stadium." Each team would consist of a guest chef plus a regularly appearing chef from the Food Network, such as Bobby Flay or Mario Batali, to serve as that team's "Iron Chef." The teams were given only sixty minutes to prepare at least five dishes based on a specific "secret" ingredient that would be revealed just before the cooking began.

In a special 90-minute episode of *Iron Chef* that aired on November 12, 2006, guest chefs Rachael Ray and Giada De Laurentiis, another chef from the Food Network, were pitted against each other. Iron Chef Bobby Flay worked with De Laurentiis while Mario Batali was paired with Rachael. The secret ingredient for the competition was cranberries.

As the only cook who was not professionally trained, Rachael said she felt a lot of pressure and was extremely nervous. She made several dishes with Batali, including shrimp served over cranberry polenta and a "drunken" pasta dish with cranberries. She also whipped up a cranberry dessert curd.

When the Cranberry Battle judging was over, no one was more shocked than Rachael herself: She and Mario Batali had won! Batali later credited Rachael's cranberry curd for their victory, saying that was what had scored them extra points. Rachael, however, found the whole thing very stressful and declared to a *Poughkeepsie Journal* reporter that she would never do it again. "It was horrible," Rachael said after the match as she bustled around the kitchen clearing plates. "Done for life. Done for life. Done for life. I like the shelter and safety of my own tiny, itty, bitty world."

OVEREXPOSED?

Rachael became a spokesperson for Dunkin' Donuts in 2007 and began shooting commercials for the company's coffee. This—along with her highly publicized appearance on *Iron Chef America*, four shows on the Food Network, a daily talk show, more than a dozen bestselling cookbooks, a food and lifestyle magazine, an extensive line of kitchen products, and her work with Nabisco—made it feel as if Rachael were everywhere. Many people felt Rachael was overexposed, an annoying "media queen" who had taken over the Food Network and was doing too many things at once.

Rachael defended her choices on several different occasions. When CNN's Larry King asked her if she felt like an industry, she responded, "No . . . I just feel like somebody who loves food." And in her interview with *Redbook*, Rachael

Rachael Ray attends a July 2007 event to promote Dunkin' Donuts iced coffee. Over the years, Rachael's popularity has also landed her endorsement jobs for Burger King and Nabisco crackers.

said she was very selective about her media appearances and the products with which she associated herself:

> I'm very picky. The knives that have my name on them are the result of my approaching the knife company for a design because I am very klutzy in the kitchen. The olive oil with my name comes from Colavita in Italy because they are related to my family. . . . I just think there's no point in limiting yourself when things are going all right.

Still, criticism of her kept coming, with a well-known, classically trained chef named Anthony Bourdain calling her a "bobble head" and expressing dismay and anger about her willingness to be a spokesperson for companies such as Dunkin' Donuts that produced unhealthy products. As reported by MSN.com, Bourdain ranted about Rachael in *Outside* magazine:

> She's got a magazine, a TV empire, all these best-selling books—I'm guessing she's not hurting for money. . . . She's hugely influential, particularly with children. It's like endorsing crack for kids. . . . Juvenile diabetes has exploded.

Again Rachael defended herself, saying that she had always enjoyed Dunkin' Donuts coffee, and that was why she'd agreed to become a spokesperson. More importantly, the company had asked her to work with its culinary team to develop healthier food and beverage items for its menu.

A YUMMY CHARITY

With her enormous cooking empire, it seemed that Rachael had already accomplished a great deal by 2007. But that was

Rachael creates at least eight or nine new recipes a week.

the year she undertook yet another huge challenge, starting the nonprofit group Yum-o!

When interviewers asked Rachael whether she and John wanted to have children, her response was always the same, that she was much too busy to be a proper parent. "I really don't have the physical energy or . . . the proper amount of time to devote . . . to having one my own," she related. Nevertheless, Rachael had always enjoyed working with children and developing special recipes for them. "I like working with children," she said, "and I love doing for children."

The very successful—and very wealthy—TV personality Oprah Winfrey had once told Rachael that when Rachael was ready to start giving back by supporting charitable efforts, she should choose something that had strong personal meaning. Now that Rachael was very wealthy herself, with an empire that was still growing, she was ready to found her own charitable organization. Remembering how much she had learned growing up in the kitchen around her mother and grandfather's cooking, she knew just what she wanted to do— help feed hungry children in the United States, and help families to develop healthy eating habits.

Rachael founded Yum-o! with that objective at its core. As stated on the organization's website, its mission is to "empower kids and their families to develop healthy relationships with food and cooking by teaching families to cook, feeding hungry kids and funding cooking education and scholarships." Rachael described this as a long-time dream in the *New York Times*:

My mom and I used to chat about how great it would be if we had some place we could teach low-income families how to stretch a buck, teach them cooking classes. . . . It's always been something I wanted to do. . . . From the time we were very small, my family always spent Thanksgiving and holiday time in the restaurant providing parties for underprivileged kids in our communities.

Yum-o! publishes plenty of family-friendly recipes on its website, teams up with partner organizations to provide food for hungry families, funds cooking programs in schools, and provides scholarship opportunities for kids who are interested in pursuing careers in the restaurant and food service industry. The organization got its name from Rachael's special word for delicious. She decided to use it for her foundation because kids often called out "Yum-o!" when they met her at book signings or media appearances. Rachael also liked the happy sound of the word, which matched her belief that food should be delicious, fun, and put a smile on people's faces.

Through Yum-o! Rachael had the opportunity to work with former president Bill Clinton, who had also devoted himself to helping kids and schools with nutritional issues. His organization Alliance for a Healthier Generation was created to fight childhood obesity, mainly by working closely with soft-drink and food manufacturers to sell healthier products in school vending machines. The organization also worked with schools that were reshaping their cafeteria and gym programs. Clinton even appeared on the *Rachael Ray* show to cook with her while talking about his own lifelong weight struggles and the dangerous rates of childhood obesity in America. While Rachael was just as concerned about kids' eating habits, her own approach was a little different, focusing primarily on how delicious and fun food can be:

> You can make any food fun food. You can make vegetables cool to a kid if you're mixing them up with something a child likes. If a kid says "What's in there?" tell them, "It's boogers and dinosaur guts." Get a giggle out of them. . . . You have to become more kid-like yourself. Think about what excites the child. It's your challenge and your job to make food cool, fun and an adventure for them.

In an effort to promote food as something that is both fun and healthy, Rachael also published a special cookbook in 2008, called *Yum-o!: The Family Cookbook*. The recipes include Rachael's own creations as well as recipes sent in by families through her website. "The recipes . . . are designed to get the whole family in the kitchen—not just around the dinner table," Rachael explained in the book's introduction. "Older kids can make the recipes all by themselves because most of them are supersimple." She also offered dozens of ways in which the "ittie bitties"—really young kids—could help out, with grown-up supervision. Depending on their abilities, for example, they could mix pancake batter, peel fruit, or grate cheese.

The first printing of *Yum-o!: The Family Cookbook* was 500,000 copies, which is about half the size of Rachael's

According to the *Every Day with Rachael Ray* website, one of Rachael's most embarrassing moments on TV was when she did a whole show with her boots on the wrong feet!

Rachael holds a copy of Yum-o! The Family Cookbook *during a May 2008 book signing. Proceeds from the cookbook go to her charitable foundation, Yum-o!*

other first printings. According to *New York Times* reporter Kim Severson, though, this is a huge number for a cookbook aimed at children, "where 20,000 is considered a strong first effort." All of the proceeds from the sales of the cookbook were donated back to the Yum-o! foundation to support more programs and activities. In Rachael's eyes this was a concrete and meaningful way she could make a difference. This comment in the *New York Times* summed up her views on the impact of teaching kids how to cook:

> It literally changes the quality of your life to . . . eat good food. It improves the nutrition of a child, and therefore it improves his or her health. But I think it's also a self-esteem issue. I think we should get our kids into the kitchen not only for their health, but because being able to provide good food for yourself is very empowering. . . . [It] feeds your soul.

VOCAL CORD SURGERY

Rachael was devoting a lot of time to her charity, but producing a daily TV show was also keeping her very busy. The *Rachael Ray* show continued to be enormously successful. In 2008 it won its first Emmy award for Outstanding Talk Show Entertainment.

That year Rachael also launched a new show called *Rachael's Vacation* on the Food Network. Another travel show, this one took viewers to vacation hotspots around the world such as Dublin, Ireland; Maui, Hawaii; and the San Juan Islands in the state of Washington. It offered lots of travel tips and suggestions for what to see and do in these fun and interesting locations.

Rachael continued working at an incredible pace, filming shows, writing cookbooks, producing the magazine, and

THE EMMY AWARDS

Emmys are TV production awards presented for different categories of the television industry: entertainment, news and documentary, and sports programming. The Primetime Emmys honor excellence in American primetime television programming, excluding sports. "Primetime" refers to the evening hours that are considered most valuable for advertising in a particular region of the country because the highest number of viewers are watching TV, for example from 8 to 11 P.M. The Daytime Emmy Awards honor excellence in American daytime television programming. The Daytime Emmys also have several categories such as Outstanding Talk Show Entertainment, Outstanding Talk Show Informative, Outstanding Children's Series, and Outstanding Performer in an Animated Program. Regional Emmys are also awarded for programming excellence within different broadcast areas throughout the country. The regional awards are important for shows that have not yet achieved a national audience.

Rachel arrives at the 38th Daytime Emmy Awards in Las Vegas, June 2010.

In 2008 and 2009 the *Rachael Ray* show won the Daytime Emmy for Outstanding Talk Show Entertainment. The show was nominated for that same award again in 2010 and 2011—as well as an additional nomination for Outstanding Talk Show Host in 2011—but did not win.

amazing many of the people around her with her nonstop energy and drive. But her voice—often called "husky" or "throaty"—sometimes gave out, leaving her with laryngitis, barely able to talk. When she learned she had a benign cyst on her vocal cord, she first tried treating it with therapy, but finally doctors recommended that she have the cyst removed with surgery. Rachael underwent the procedure in 2009. It was considered minor surgery, but it came with some challenges. Afterward, Rachael had to rest her voice for nearly three weeks—no easy feat for a talkative person who also happened to be the star of a hugely successful daytime talk show!

Fortunately, the treatment was successful. It not only cured her persistent laryngitis problem, it also led to a brand-new devotion to fitness. Out of boredom during her recovery, she took up jogging. "I used to say I would never run unless I was being chased by someone with a gun," she joked in *People* magazine. "Now I'm a little obsessed with it!"

Soon she was working out, too, heading to a local gym with her husband six mornings a week and fitting into jeans that were two sizes smaller. She told *People* magazine, "I feel more fit . . . and I have a little more energy—which is ridiculous because I have five jobs! So obviously I already have a good amount of energy!"

THE ANIMAL LOVER

None of this activity took away from Rachael's desire to make a difference in the world. Helping children through Yum-o! was not the only cause that Rachael considered near and dear to her heart. A lifetime animal lover, Rachael also wanted to use her money and influence to help mistreated animals. She added a Rachael's Rescue page to her official websites to spotlight groups that help people adopt stray

In June 2008, Rachael won the Emmy Award for Outstanding Talk Show Entertainment. The show would win the same award in 2009.

pets. She also supported Bad Rap, an organization dedicated to providing education about pit bulls. An interview in *Time Magazine for Kids* helped explain her interest in animal charities:

> I have a pit bull, and pit bulls are very misunderstood. They're frequently tortured and sent to fight each other. I started out just wanting to help pit bulls, but as my business grew, we realized we had the ability to help out all animals. So far, we've raised about $1.5 million.

Another way Rachael felt she could help animals was by creating a new brand of pet food. The Rachael Ray Nutrish product line included healthy pet foods and snacks made from natural ingredients. A portion of the proceeds from the pet food sales were donated to the pet adoption groups spotlighted on the Rachael's Rescue web page.

CHAPTER EIGHT

LIFE TODAY

By the end of 2008, Rachael was a multimillionaire. But in many ways she still felt and acted like a regular person—a "hick from the sticks" as she called herself, who often shopped at inexpensive retail stores and drank "beer and not champagne." No matter how much money she made or how famous she became, she still identified most strongly with ordinary working people.

A RECESSION

When a serious economic recession struck that year, many businesses and retail shops across America began downsizing or even closing. It also affected restaurants and food stores as well as the business of food publishing. A very highly regarded food magazine, *Gourmet*, was shut down in 2009 by its parent company, Conde Nast. The upscale publication had been operating since 1941 and was considered by many to be the best food magazine on the market.

Rachael and others around her were aware that the recession might impact the sales of her own products, including

Rachael scoops gelato at an event to promote the newly launched Cooking Channel, 2011. Her philosophy of keeping things simple and sweet has helped Rachael maintain her position as one of the most popular celebrity chefs.

the magazine and cookbooks. There were some signs of trouble at *Every Day with Rachael Ray* as well, with a bit of staff turnover and less involvement from Rachael, who was focusing more on the *Rachael Ray* show and her charity work.

In a *Nightline* interview, though, Rachael said that she thought her business was "built for recession." In hard economic times, she believed, her recipes and approach to food and lifestyle issues were more relevant than ever:

> The magazine, the daytime show, we've always tried to write affordable, accessible [recipes]. . . . Those are key words for us, and I do mean us, a huge staff of people at the magazine who love to cook affordable, friendly food that helps families eat better for less. So I think this is really a time for all of our team to shine. . . . You know, food is . . . a hug for people.

A few industry analysts echoed Rachael's words, saying that the cooking business had become more democratic since the rise of Rachael and some other chefs on the Food Network. According to a *New York Times* article on the closing of *Gourmet*, people were no longer interested in elite publications such as *Gourmet* with upscale and inaccessible recipes. They could not afford the sometimes expensive ingredients and had less and less time available to look for those ingredients in specialized food markets—or to fuss over very detailed preparation instructions. As reporter

One of Rachael's favorite sayings is "K.I.S.S.—Keep It Super Simple!"

Stephanie Clifford commented, "What harried cooks want now, it seems, is less a distant idol and more a pal."

THE ANTI-MARTHA STEWART

With her laid-back approach to cooking, Rachael clearly fit that description of viewers' "pal" in the kitchen. It was not surprising that she was often contrasted with another TV personality—cookbook author and lifestyle expert Martha Stewart. Like Rachael, Martha Stewart's career was devoted to showing Americans how to cook and entertain. Stewart had also hosted her own TV shows as well as publishing food and lifestyle magazines and dozens of cookbooks.

While Martha Stewart's recipes aimed for elegance and sophistication, Rachael's overall approach to cooking was much simpler and more down-home. "You can do it" is the message she most wanted to convey to people. "To her credit, Ray has always cast herself as a sort of anti-Martha," wrote Jill Hunter Pellettieri in *Slate* magazine, "offering options for those who want to save money, eat healthfully, and cook at home but don't have the time or budget to entertain [in an elaborate] way.

In a 2009 appearance on *Nightline*, Martha Stewart had some critical words for Rachael, as reported in *US* magazine:

> Well, to me, [Rachael] professed that she [cannot] bake. . . . [She] just did a new cookbook which is just a re-edit of a lot of her old recipes. [And] that's not good enough for me. . . . [Ray is] more of an entertainer . . . with her bubbly personality, than she is a teacher, like me.

Rachael responded in her typical unassuming way. "Why would it make me mad," she said when asked if

Stewart's remarks made her angry. "Her skill set is far beyond mine. . . . That doesn't mean that what I do isn't important too. . . . I really just think she's being honest. She does have a better skill set than I do when it comes to producing a beautiful, perfect, high-quality meal. . . . I'd rather eat Martha's than mine, too."

Clearly, TV executives continued to see Rachael as a "pal" in the kitchen with an appealing "can-do" message. In 2009 the *Rachael Ray* show received another Emmy Award for Best Talk Show—Entertainment, and the network renewed the show through the year 2012. When she accepted the Emmy that year, Rachael was humble, mentioning the difficult economic conditions for many Americans at the time. "I'm just thankful to have a job in the recession and be working," she said in *People* magazine.

THE COOKING CHANNEL

The Food Network launched a spinoff channel in 2010 called the Cooking Channel. This one was "targeted at a hipper crowd," according to the *New York Times*: "The feel and style [they were] going for [was] a little grittier, a little edgier, a little hipper." There were some brand-new shows, including *Unique Eats* and an unusual show, *Food Jammers*, that featured three young mechanics who built odd devices such as vending machines for tacos. Some of the established chefs from the Food Network were offered shows on the Cooking Channel. The title of Rachael's new program was *Rachael Ray's Week in a Day*. As described on the Cooking Channel website, "The woman who taught America how to make a meal in 30 minutes is back with an even bigger promise: one day of cooking, up to five days of eating!" Each episode showed viewers how to prepare five

The syndicated Rachael Ray *show remains one of the most popular daytime programs.* Rachael Ray *has a daily viewing audience of about 2.6 million, making it one of the highest viewed daytime shows.*

Rachael Ray poses with fellow Food Network chef Guy Fieri. Their show Guy vs. Rachael's Celebrity Cook-off *began airing in early 2012.*

meals in a single day so that the food would be ready in advance for the whole week.

In 2011 the Food Network announced plans for yet another new show featuring Rachael and fellow celebrity chef Guy Fieri, the host of *Diners, Drive-ins, and Dives*. This new show was a cooking competition called *Guy vs. Rachael's Celebrity Cook-off*. Rachael described the show as "the cooking equivalent of *Dancing With the Stars*." Guy Fieri added, "We're going to get some celebrities that come on the show with different levels of culinary technique. . . . Rachael's going to get [four], I'm going to get [four] and it's going to be battle royale!"

IN THE DIGITAL AGE

Many more new opportunities arose through the growing popularity of electronic media. Rachael had already launched some new electronic products, including e-versions of her cookbooks as well as her magazine, *Every Day with Rachael Ray*. In 2010 she launched a new iPhone and iPad application. Called "Tasty Bytes," the app had two hundred recipes along with some cooking tips and a shopping tool to help users shop for the ingredients they needed. Rachael explained that she had decided to develop the app mainly for convenience:

> When I head to the grocery store, I know what meals I want to make for the week and I buy ingredients based on those recipes. . . . I figured why not create a recipe database that was portable and mobile, so I could provide busy cooks, including myself, with a simple way to search through tons of recipes and be able to shop for ingredients in the fastest way possible.

That year Rachael also entered into a partnership with Demand Media, Inc., a content and social media company.

JULIA CHILD

Rachael has often been compared to another famous female chef, Julia Child, who was one of the first women to cook on TV. Born in California in 1912, Child moved to France with her husband, Paul, in 1948. After eating a delicious French meal of oysters and sole meuniere, she became entranced by French food and the idea that food could open up a person's soul and spirit. Soon she enrolled in a famous cooking school—Le Cordon Bleu—and began writing a cookbook with two other women. *Mastering the Art of French Cooking* was published in 1961 and quickly became a bestseller, showing many Americans for the first time how to prepare fine French foods. In 1963 Child began demonstrating French cooking on her popular TV show, *The French Chef.* Like Rachael, she was known for making cooking fun and accessible.

Rachael was named "the lead creative force" for Demand Media's eHow Food channel, an online resource that publishes information related to issues such as health, money, and food. Rachael's job was to identify and then develop up-and-coming culinary talent for the website.

MORE CHARITY WORK

Rachael's position and wealth also enabled her to continue devoting time and money to charities. In 2010 Rachael announced that she would be donating $775,000 to support organizations that helped animals, bringing the total amount donated from her proceeds to more than $1.4 million. "It truly brings a smile to my face," she said, "to know that this money will help so many animals who just need someone to care for them."

Rachael continued to work tirelessly to improve the nutritional life of children and families. She helped the New York City schools provide healthier meals for students, developing a new chicken taco dish and persuading the schools' cafeterias to use whole wheat pasta in their macaroni and cheese. She traveled to Washington, D.C., to appear before Congress with New York State senator Kirsten Gillibrand to discuss the federal government's reimbursement rates for school lunches. Like Senator Gillibrand, Rachael was outraged by what she felt were very

Once for his birthday, John asked Rachael to make pasta carbonara—a simple pasta dish made with cream, eggs, Parmesan cheese, and bacon bits. Rachael says that's when she knew she'd marry him one day!

Rachael prepares a meal on her hit Cooking Channel show Rachael Ray's Week in a Day. *"The whole idea of the show is that you cook for one day and you get five nights of meals that are already fully cooked," she explained." You just go home and heat them up in one way or another. You do one day's worth of grocery shopping, and then you go home and you cook on your day off."*

low rates of reimbursement. Together the women argued that the rate of reimbursement should be increased by seventy cents per child. In a *New York Times* article about her visit to Capitol Hill, Rachael expressed her frustration with the lack of federal funding:

> How could you go to any state in the union and say you are not for an extra couple of cents to eradicate hunger, to make our kids healthier, stronger, better focused. . . . It doesn't make any sense that you would even have to have a long conversation about that, to me.

As she put it, she was using her "big Sicilian mouth" to heighten awareness of the importance of feeding children well and teaching them good nutritional habits. And her visit may have helped. Seven months later, President Barack Obama signed a bill expanding access to free lunch programs.

LIFE TODAY

The year 2010 was a very big one for Rachael overall. She celebrated several significant anniversaries: her five-year wedding anniversary, five years of producing her syndicated daytime show *Rachael Ray*, and ten years of being affiliated with the Food Network. That year she also published her eighteenth cookbook.

Today Rachael's mom Elsa still lives in Rachael's cabin, which she has transformed into an elaborate Italian garden with paved stone paths. She also answers Rachael's fan mail.

Today Rachael and John own several homes, including an apartment in New York City's Greenwich Village and a house in the Hamptons on eastern Long Island. At least once a month they retreat to the cabin in the Adirondacks, where Rachael has made some changes over the years, such as purchasing the three and half acres of land adjacent to the cabin so she could "will it forever wild." She also used reclaimed barn wood from all over New York State to build a larger kind of

Rachel and John attend a 2010 event.

gathering place on the cabin grounds. But in many ways the cabin looks just as it did years ago when it was her main residence. "I live in the same place, I have the same furniture. I shop the same grocery store," she said. "I move through the world the same way I always have. I have a lot more continuity in my life than people might imagine."

When Rachael is in New York City, she and John also like to live simply, staying home, watching movies and cooking meals together. She explained this in *Good Housekeeping*, saying, "I'm happiest at home when I'm curled up in bed with

Rachael further extended her reach by sponsoring and hosting a special concert at the 2010 music and arts festival South By Southwest. Rachael's show featured food and drink tastings as well as a performance from her husband's band.

my dog, Isaboo, and my hubby watching a movie or eating Sunday brunch."

As for the future, it's certain to bring more new opportunities and successes her way. But she herself is not spending a lot of time worrying about what will happen next. "You can spend so much time planning ahead or having a two-year plan or a five-year plan, but life has a funny way of changing that," she shared. "So I don't know what's going to happen." In fact, Rachael sees her life as "a total accident—a very happy, wonderful accident that I didn't and couldn't have planned."

Others who know Rachael, however, see her success as no surprise at all—something that has come as a direct result of her cooking talents and an incredible work ethic. "Day one, we knew that she was just going somewhere and doing something," said her sister Maria. "She's always risen to the top." Her father added, "She's the hardest-working person I know."

Despite all the complications that have come with Rachael's celebrity, wealth, and hectic lifestyle, in the end her life boils down to something very simple: a firm belief in the essential importance and richness of eating good food. She once explained this belief in this way:

> That is what is so easy about my job. I am sharing the idea that just learning how to make a few simple dishes for yourself or with your kids or for your friends . . . not only improves the quality of your life, it improves the quality of the lives of those you choose to share the food with. It just does.

While Rachael's critics are likely to continue voicing complaints about everything from her cutesy catchphrases to her clothes to her lack of professional training, she still has millions of very loyal fans. In 2011, Rachael even received the People's Choice Award for Favorite TV Chef, with votes coming from regular people rather than industry insiders. As far as anyone can tell, Rachael Ray is here to stay!

p. 8:   "She was just this really . . ." "Rachael Ray," Biography.com. http://www.biography.com/articles/Rachael-Ray-201254.

p. 8:   "I was so scared when . . . " Ibid.

p. 8:   "Al Roker! . . ." Ibid.

p. 10: "Of all the soups . . ." Jeff Pearlman, "Rachael Ray's 16 Secrets for Entertaining in Style, *TV Guide* (December 21, 2006). http://www.everythingrachaelray.com/2006/12/rachael-revisits-her-past-with-tv-guide.html.

p. 10: "smiling from ear to ear . . ." Laura Jacobs, "Just Say Yum-O," *Vanity Fair* (September 11, 2007). http://www.vanityfair.com/culture/features/2007/10/rachaelray20071.

p. 10: "like a fairy tale . . ." Deborah Roberts and Katie Thomson, "Rachael Ray's Sizzling Success Story" (Sept. 19, 2006). http://abcnews.go.com/2020/story?id=2460303page=2.

p. 11: "What am I doing . . ." Karu F. Daniels, "Rachael Ray: Developing Story," *AOL Black Voices* (May 1, 2007). http://www.bvnewswire.com/2007/05/01/rachael-ray-story-developing/.

p. 12: "[My mom] brought us . . ." Tara Parker-Pope, "Rachael Ray Wants Kids in the Kitchen," *New York Times* (September 14, 2008). http://well.blogs.nytimes.com/2008/09/14/rachael-ray-wants-kids-in-the-kitchen/.

p. 13: "My first vivid memory . . ." Biography on Rachaelray.com. http://www.rachaelray.com/rach/bio.php.

p. 14: "play music and . . ." Rachael Ray, *Cooking Rocks! Rachael Ray 30-Minute Meals for Kids* (New York: Lake Isle Press, 2004), p. 8.

p. 14: "The minute she was up . . ." Jacobs, "Just Say Yum-o."

p. 14: "good food . . . garlic and oil." Biography.com.

p. 15: "drawing something . . ." Jacobs, "Just Say Yum-o."

p. 16: "I had the lunchbox . . ." Paul Chi, "Rachael Ray: 'I Sat Alone in the Cafeteria,'" *People* (December 7, 2007). http://www.people.com/people/article/0,,20164849,00.html.

p. 16: "I don't want to do . . ." Jacobs, "Just Say Yum-o."

p. 17: "I'm a pale comparison . . ." Roberts and Thompson, "Rachael Ray's Sizzling Success Story."

p. 17: "I was surrounded . . ." Biography on Rachaelray.com

p. 17: "The kitchen was the center . . ." Ray, *Cooking Rocks!*, p. 6.

p. 18: "For us, it made for . . ." "Rachael Ray," The Internet Movie Database (IMDb). http://www.imdb.com/name/nm1301904.

p. 18: "ta-da cheerleader . . ." John Marshall, "Rachael Ray's Energy and

Success Keep Her Going and Going," *Seattle Post-Intelligencer* (December 17, 2006). http://www.seattlepi.com/default/article/Rachael-Ray-s-energy-and-success-keep-her-going-1222562.php.

p. 21:   "It felt . . ." Jacobs, "Just Say Yum-o."

p. 22:   "I saw this little ad . . ." Ibid.

p. 24:   "We had a problem . . ." Biography.com.

p. 25:   "Nothing much happened. . ." Jacobs, "Just Say Yum-o."

p. 26:   "She was a workaholic . . ." Ibid.

p. 27:   "If people will wait . . ." Ibid.

p. 27:   "Who cares? . . ." Ibid.

p. 29:   "We had everyone from Girl Scouts . . ." Rachael Ray, "My Journey to the Top," *Newsweek* (October 9, 2007). http://www.newsweek.com/2007/10/09/my-journey-to-the-top.html.

p. 29:   "it made for a really . . ." Biography.com.

p. 31:   "Rachael said, 'If I don't . . ." Jacobs, "Just Say Yum-o."

p. 31:   "It was check-to-check . . ." David A. Keeps, "Rachael Ray's Rules for a Delicious Life," *Good Housekeeping* (July 2010). http://www.goodhousekeeping.com/family/celebrity/rachael-ray-biography.

p. 33:   "People started writing me . . ." Ray, "My Journey to the Top."

p. 34:   "That's impossible! . . ." Biography.com.

p. 34:   "Change recipes to reflect . . ." Rachael Ray, *30-Minute Meals* (New York: Lake Isle Press, 1998), pp. 21–23.

p. 34:   "You taught me . . ." Ibid., p. 5.

p. 35:   "My mom and I . . ." Ray, "My Journey to the Top."

p. 36:   "knack for spotting hosts . . ." Allen Salkin, "Newcomer to Food Television Tries for a Little Grit," *New York Times* (April 21, 2010). http://www.nytimes.com/2010/04/21/dining/21network.html.

p. 36:   "I watched her . . ." Biography.com.

p. 38:   "I said, 'Listen, . . ." Jacobs, "Just Say Yum-o."

p. 38:   "Rachael came along . . ." Ibid.

p. 39:   "She's got a big, big personality . . ." Ibid.

p. 39:   "What's interesting is . . ." Ibid.

p. 41:   "Ray leapt into television . . ." Beth Silcox, "Keeping it Real," *Success*, http://www.successmagazine.com/keeping-it-real/PARAMS/article/1344/channel/22.

p. 42:   "electrified audiences" Biography.com

p. 42:   "She is a world-class . . ." Keeps, "Rachael Ray's Rules for a Delicious Life."

p. 45:   "I was raised . . ." Holly Taylor, "Rachael Ray Can't Stop Talking," *Redbook* 207, 207, no. 4 (October 2006), p. 60.

p. 45:   "I was taping, and they . . ." Dan Snierson, "Stupid Questions with Rachael Ray," *Entertainment Weekly* (October 13, 2006).

http://www.ew.com/ew/article/0,,1545622,00.html.

p. 47:   "She single-handedly changed . . ." Jacobs, "Just Say Yum-o."

p. 47:   "quite active in posting . . ." Rob Walker, "Anti-Fan Club." *New York Times* (November 26, 2006). http://www.nytimes.com /2006/11/26/magazine/26wwln_consumed.html.

p. 47:   "They can't stand the way . . ." Biography.com.

p. 48:   "The show is fantastically . . ." Jill Pellettieri, "Rachael Ray: Why Food Snobs Should Quit Picking on Her," *Slate* (July 13, 2005). http://www.slate.com/id/2122085/.

p. 48:   "As [Rachael] became more . . ." Ibid.

p. 48:   "Her Super Sloppy Joes . . ." Ibid.

p. 49:   "Most of what they say . . ." Jacobs, "Just Say Yum-o."

p. 49:   "What am I going to do? . . ." Keeps, "Rachael Ray's Rules for a Delicious Life."

p. 50:   "I can't really . . ." Taylor, "Rachael Ray Can't Stop Talking," p. 60.

p. 50:   "I don't think Rachael Ray . . ." Biography.com.

p. 50:   "She's a machine . . ." Kim Severson, "Being Rachael Ray: How Cool is That?" *New York Times* (October 19, 2005). http://www.nytimes.com/2005/10/19/dining/19rach.html.

p. 50:   "She and I have words . . ." Ibid.

p. 51:   "My very good friend . . ." Larry King, "Interview with Rachael Ray," *CNN* (September 18, 2006). http://archives.cnn.com/TRANSCRIPTS/0609/18/lkl.01.html.

p. 53:   "clean pots and dishes . . ." Ray, *Cooking Rocks!*, p. 17.

p. 53:   "small heavy skillets are handy . . ." Ibid., p. 21.

p. 53:   "To cool kids everywhere . . ." Ibid., p. 3.

p. 53:   "I won't allow the books . . ." Jacobs, "Just Say Yum-o."

p. 53:   "The recipes can't require . . ." John Marshall, "Rachael Ray's Energy and Success Keep Her Going and Going," *Seattle Post-Intelligencer* (December 17, 2006). http://www.seattlepi.com/default/article/Rachael-Ray-s-energy-and-success-keep-her-going-1222562.php.

p. 55:   "Rachael has a long memory . . ." Keeps, "Rachael Ray's Rules for a Delicious Life."

p. 55:   "I thought if I'm gutsy . . ." Cynthia McFadden and Sarah Rosenberg, "Rachael Ray: 'I Don't Regret a Thing." *ABC News Nightline* (March 2, 2009). http://abcnews.go.com/Nightline /Recipes/rachael-ray-regret-thing/story?id=6976299.

p. 56:   "It was the most scared . . ." Ibid.

p. 56:   "I can't give a man . . ." Liza Hamm and Michelle Tauber, "Rachael Ray's Recipe for Marriage," *People* (May 2, 2007). http://www.peo-ple.com/people/article/0,,20037511,00.html.

p. 58:   "That was the stupidest idea . . ." Severson, "Being Rachael Ray: How Cool is That?"

p. 59: "I want to see . . ." Lia Miller, "From Food Network to the Magazine Rack," *New York Times* (April 25, 2005). http://query.nytimes.com/gst/fullpage.html?res=9C07E4D91531F936A15757C0A9639C8B63.

p. 60: "The dog was so high energy . . ." "Rachael Ray 'Tails Inc.' Cover Features Pit Bull Love," *Vegetarian Star* (October 15, 2010). http://vegetarianstar.com/2010/10/15/rachael-ray-tails-inc-cover-features-pit-bull-love/.

p. 62: "They're some of the . . ." King, "Interview with Rachael Ray."

p. 62: "I came home from work, . . ." Jacobs, "Just Say Yum-o."

p. 63: "In order to do . . ." "Rachael Ray Has a Lot on her Plate," *Time* (Sept. 5, 2006). www.time.com/time/magazine/article/0,9171,1531337,00.html.

p. 64: "Everything in the show . . ." Taylor, "Rachael Ray Can't Stop Talking," p. 60.

p. 64: "We want the normal people . . ." Olivia Barker, "Ray Keeps Her Sunny Side Up," *USA Today* (September 13, 2006). http://www.usatoday.com/life/television/news/2006-09-13-rachael-ray_x.htm.

p. 64: "There's a lot of viewer involvement . . ." King, "Interview with Rachael Ray."

p. 65: "She's like everybody. . . ." Barker, "Ray Keeps Her Sunny Side Up."

p. 65: "debuted with . . ." Jim Benson, "Rachael Ray Rules in Ratings," *Broadcasting & Cable* (October 3, 2006). http://www.broadcastingcable.com/article/print/106003-Rachael_Ray_Rules_in_Ratings.php.

p. 65: "I was so nervous . . ." King, "Interview with Rachael Ray."

p. 65: "main attribute was . . ." "Rachael Ray Has a Lot on her Plate," *Time*.

p. 66: "All of our walls here . . ." Taylor, "Rachael Ray Can't Stop Talking," p. 60.

p. 66: "Ms. Ray's first show . . ." Alessandra Stanley, "Beyond the Kitchen, Breaking Bread with America," *New York Times* (September 19, 2006). http://tv.nytimes.com/2006/09/19/arts/television/19stan.html.

p. 67: "have had no impact on . . ." Walker, "Anti-Fan Club."

p. 67: "If you've got a fan base . . ." Ibid.

p. 67: "exploding, with a promised . . ." David Carr, "Rachael Ray Gives the Gift of Time," *New York Times* (October 23, 2006). http://query.nytimes.com/gst/fullpage.html?res=9C02E2DD173FF930A15753C1A9609C8B63.

p. 67: "I just showed [people] . . ." Biography.com.

p. 67: "I felt like I was going . . ." Ibid.

p. 68: "In fewer than five years, . . ." Mario Batali, "Rachael Ray," *Time* (April 30, 2006). http://www.time.com/time/magazine/article/0,9171,1187293,00.html.

p. 70: "It was horrible, . . . " Everythingrachaelray.com (November 9, 2006). http://www.everythingrachaelray.com/2006/11/tv-alert-iron-chef-america_09.html.

p. 70: "No . . . I just feel like . . ." King, "Interview with Rachael Ray."

p. 72: "I'm very picky. . . ." John Marshall, "Rachael Ray's Energy and Success Keep Her Going and Going."

p. 72: "She's got a magazine, . . ." "Anthony Bourdain dunks evil Rachael Ray," MSN.com. (October 12, 2007). http://today.msnbc.msn.com/id/21255843/ns/today-today_entertainment/t/anthony-bourdain-dunks-evil-rachael-ray/.

p. 73: "I really don't have . . ." King, "Interview with Rachael Ray."

p. 73: "empower kids and their families . . ." "What is Yum-o!," Yum.org, http://www.yum-o.org/what_is.php.

p. 74: "My mom and I used . . ." Tara Parker-Pope, "Rachael Ray Wants Kids in the Kitchen."

p. 75: "You can make any food . . ." Ibid.

p. 75: "The recipes . . . are designed . . ." Rachael Ray, *Yum-o!: the Family Cookbook* (New York: Clarkson Potter, 2008), p. 10.

p. 77: "where 20,000 is considered . . ." Kim Severson, "Cookbook Publishers Try to Think Small," *New York Times* (May 14, 2008). http://www.nytimes.com/2008/05/14/dining/14kids.html?.

p. 77: "It literally changes the quality . . ." Tara Parker-Pope, "Rachael Ray Wants Kids in the Kitchen."

p. 79: "I used to say . . ." Liza Hamm, "Rachael Ray: How I Lost Two Jeans Sizes," *People* (October 5, 2009). http://www.people.com/people/archive/article/0,,20314202,00.html.

p. 79: "I feel more fit . . ." Ibid.

p. 81: "I have a pit bull, . . ." Francesco Franzese, "Rachael Ray's Pet Project," *Time for Kids* (December 30, 2010). http://www.time-forkids.com/TFK/kids/news/story/0,28277,2039351,00.html.

p. 84: "built for recession," McFadden and Rosenberg, "Rachael Ray: 'I Don't Regret a Thing.'"

p. 84: "The magazine, the daytime show, . . ." Ibid.

p. 85: "What harried cooks want . . ." Stephanie Clifford, "Conde Nast Closes *Gourmet* and 3 Other Magazines" *New York Times* (October 6, 2009). http://www.nytimes.com/2009/10/06/business/media/06gourmet.html.

p. 85: "To her credit, . . ." Pellettieri, "Rachael Ray: Why Food Snobs Should Quit Picking on Her."

p. 85: "Well, to me, . . ." "Martha Stewart Slams Rachael Ray," *US* (November 18, 2009). http://www.usmagazine.com/celebritynews/news/martha-stewart-slams-rachael-ray-20091811.

p. 85: "Why would it make . . ." Ibid.

p. 86: "I'm just thankful . . ." Stephen M. Silverman, "Rachael Ray Wins Daytime Emmy for Best Talk Show," *People* (August 31, 2009). http://www.people.com/people/article/0,,20301377,00.html.

p. 86:   "targeted at a hipper crowd . . ." Salkin, "Newcomer to Food
           Television Tries for a Little Grit."

p. 86:   "The woman who taught America . . ." Cookingchannel.com,
           http://www.cookingchanneltv.com/rachael-rays-week-in-a-
           day/index.html.

p. 88:   "the cooking equivalent . . ." "On the Show," Rachaelrayshow.com,
           http://www.rachaelrayshow.com/show/segments/view/guy-fieri/.

p. 89:   "When I head to . . ." Michelle Locke, "Rachael Ray has an App
           for You," *Miami Herald* (August 19, 2010). http://www.miamiher-
           ald.com
           /2010/08/19/1781371/rachael-ray-has-an-app-for-you.html.

p. 90:   "It truly brings a smile . . ." Rachaelrayshow.com,
           http://www.rachaelray.com/article.php?article_id=288&section=news.

p. 91:   "The whole idea of the show . . ." Erin Renzas, "Rachael Ray
           Dishes on Her New Show" iVillage Food (October 20, 2010).
           http://www.ivillage.com/rachael-ray-week-day/3-a-291538

p. 92:   "How could you go . . ." Michael Barbaro, "Rachael Ray and
           Senator Lobby for School Lunch," *New York Times* (May 11, 2010).
           http://www.nytimes.com/2010/05/12/nyregion/12food.html.

p. 93:   "will it forever wild" Patricia Sheridan, "Patricia Sheridan's
           Breakfast With . . . Rachael Ray," *Pittsburgh Post-Gazette*
           (November 22, 2010). http://www.post-gazette.com/pg
           /10326/1104813-129.stm.

p. 93:   "I live in the same . . ." Ibid.

p. 93:   "I'm happiest at home . . ." Keeps, "Rachael Ray's Rules for a
           Delicious Life."

p. 94:   "You can spend so much . . ." Sheridan, "Patricia Sheridan's
           Breakfast With . . . Rachael Ray."

p. 94:   "a total accident . . ." Biography on Rachaelray.com.

p. 94:   "Day one . . ." Jacobs, "Just Say Yum-o!"

p. 95:   "She's the hardest-working . . ." Ibid.

p. 95:   "That is what is . . ." Ray, "My Journey to the Top."

1968: Rachael Ray was born on August 25 on Cape Cod, Massachusetts.

1986: Rachael graduates from Lake George High School and enrolls at Pace University.

1991: Rachael moves to New York City.

1993: The gourmet food store Agata & Valentina hires Rachael as a manager and buyer.

1995: Rachael moves back to upstate New York and begins working at Cowan & Lobel as a food buyer.

1996: Rachael teaches her first "30-Minute Meal" class at Cowan & Lobel.

1997: Rachael begins doing cooking segments on WRGB-TV.

1997: Rachael's segments are nominated for two local Emmy awards.

1998: Rachael's first cookbook, *30-Minute Meals*, is published by Lake Isle Press.

2001: In March, Rachael appears on the *Today* show. In November, the show *30-Minute Meals* debuts on the Food Network.

2002: Rachael's travel show, *$40 a Day*, debuts on the Food Network.

2003: The *Rachael Ray* brand of kitchen products is launched.

2005: Rachael marries John Cusimano in Tuscany, Italy. The magazine *Every Day with Rachael Ray* begins publication.

2006: *Time* names Rachael one of "100 People who Shape Our World." *Rachael Ray*, a daytime talk show, debuts. Rachael wins the Cranberry Battle on *Iron Chef America*.

2007: Rachael starts the Yum-o! foundation to improve children's nutrition and eating habits.

2008: The *Rachael Ray* show wins a Daytime Emmy award for Outstanding Talk Show.

2009: *Rachael Ray* wins another Emmy and is renewed through 2012.

2010: Rachael's Vacation debuts on the Cooking Channel. "Tasty Bytes," an iPhone and iPad app, is launched.

2011: Rachael Ray receives another Emmy Award nomination. Rachael wins a People's Choice Awards for Favorite TV Chef.

CAJUN CUISINE—a country style of cooking that combines French and Southern cuisines. Cajun dishes are generally very spicy and often involve cooking with pork fat. Jambalaya is a typical Cajun dish.

CALAMARI—cooked squid, usually sliced into rings and fried with a batter coating.

CHUTNEY—a spicy condiment that is made with fruit, vinegar, sugar and spices. It ranges in texture from smooth to chunky.

CREOLE CUISINE—a type of cooking that is very similar to Cajun and influenced by French, Spanish, and African cooking. Creole cooking uses more butter and cream and less animal fat than Cajun. Gumbo is a popular Creole dish.

CULINARY—related to cooking or the kitchen

CURD—a creamy mixture made from a citrus juice (such as lemon or lime), sugar, butter, and egg yolks. Often used as a topping for breads and other baked goods.

CYST—an abnormal sac that develops somewhere on the body; some cysts must be removed with surgery.

GELATO—a very rich, soft Italian ice cream.

GORGONZOLA—a type of Italian blue cheese often served in salads or with fruit.

GOURMET—high-quality food that is carefully prepared.

HAUTE CUISINE—food that is prepared and presented in an elegant and artful manner.

JAMBALAYA—a rice and meat stew seasoned with tomatoes and herbs.

PIEROGIES—Polish dumplings often filled with mashed potatoes, pork, onions, or other seasonings.

POLENTA—boiled ground cornmeal often served as a side dish.

PREMIERE—a debut or first performance.

SARDINE—a small, salty fish.

SELF-DEPRECATING—humble or acting in a manner that minimizes one's skills or accomplishments.

SOLE MEUNIERE—a French dish in which sole, a type of fish, is seasoned, lightly dusted with flour, then sautéed in butter.

SOURDOUGH—a bread with a sour, tangy flavor that results from the special ingredients used to make the bread rise.

FURTHER READING

Abrams, Dennis. *Rachael Ray: Food Entrepreneur.* New York: Chelsea House Publishers, 2008.

Carle, Meghan, Jill Carle, and Judi Carle. *Teens Cook: How to Cook What You Want to Eat.* Berkeley, CA: Ten Speed Press, 2011.

Jango-Cohen, Judith. *The History of Food.* Minneapolis, MN: Twenty-First Century Books, 2006.

Ray, Rachael, and Chris Kalb. *Cooking Rocks! Rachael Ray 30-Minute Meals for Kids.* New York: Lake Isle Press, 2004.

Ray, Rachael. *Kid Food: Rachael Ray's Top 30 30-Minute Meals.* New York: Lake Isle Press, 2005.

Ray, Rachael. *Yum-O!: The Family Cookbook.* New York: Clarkson Potter, 2008.

INTERNET RESOURCES

WWW.COOKINGCHANNELTV.COM

The official website of the Food Network's Cooking Channel includes a biography of Rachael Ray as well as general information about its other shows and hosts. The site also features cooking videos and recipes.

WWW.FOODNETWORK.COM/RACHAEL-RAY/INDEX.HTML

Rachael Ray's pages on the Food Network's website include some of her top recipes and information about her various shows. The Food Network site also includes recipes and some kid-friendly cooking information.

WWW.KIDSACOOKIN.KSU.EDU

This website features a special recipe of the week, plus cooking tips and a fun poll section where visitors can vote on their favorite foods.

WWW.RACHAELRAY.COM

Rachael Ray's official site includes information about her background, TV shows, books, and cookware. Several pages on the site are devoted to her animal rescue efforts as well as her Yum-o! foundation.

WWW.YUM-O.ORG

Information and recent news about Rachael's foundation for promoting healthy eating and food education. Also includes games, recipes, and activities for kids.

INDEX

Numbers in **bold italics** refer to captions.

CONTRIBUTORS

SUSAN KORMAN is the author of more than thirty books for children. She has worked as an editor, writer, and school librarian. She lives in Bucks County, Pennsylvania, with her husband and three children.